As Nature Leads

As Nature Leads

An informal discussion of the reason why Negro
and Caucasian are mixing in spite of
opposition

BY

J. A. ROGERS

Author of "FROM SUPERMAN TO MAN"

———

DEDICATED TO THE MEMORY OF HIRAM H. HOLLAND, MY
MORE THAN BROTHER, WHOSE YOUTHFUL DEATH
DEPRIVED THE NEGRO RACE OF ONE OF ITS
RICHEST AND GENTLEST SOULS.

Black Classic Press
P.O. Box 13414
Baltimore, MD 21203
1987

"*Our race is essentially slavish; it is the nature of all of us to believe blindly in what we love, rather than that which is most wise. We are inclined to look upon an honest, unshrinking pursuit of truth as something irreverent. We are indignant when others pry into our idols and criticise them with impunity, just as a savage flies to arms when a missionary picks his fetish to pieces. . . .*

The mass of mankind plods on with eyes fixed in the footsteps of the generations that went before, too indifferent or too fearful to raise their glances to judge for themselves whether the path they are traveling is the best or to learn the conditions by which they are surrounded and affected."

GALTON.

PREFACE.

My first care and most pleasant duty must be to thank those friends who, when I left the firstling of my literary offspring, a forlorn and shivering infant on the steps of the Sisters Three, gathered it up, and so energetically and so unselfishly fostered its growth, inadequate and feeble though I know that anything I ever could say would be. These friends, many of whom I still eagerly hope to meet in person, have been many, and I could not hope to mention them individually; I therefore must most regretfully limit myself to specifically thanking some of the principal ones, bearing at the same time the liveliest, if silent, gratitude to the others.

Among the earliest, indeed the discoverers of whatever worth there is in the volume, are Mrs. N. T. Myers, Superintendent of Kindergarten at Washington, D. C.; Miss E. F. G. Merrit, Superintendent of Primary, and Mrs. Rachel Guy Moore, also an instructor in the same city. These ladies, without having known me, labored in and out of season, unremuneratedly, to circulate it. Mrs. Moore disposed of nearly the whole second edition, buying books with the commission earned and presenting them to influential persons. To others of my Washington friends I must add the name of Mr. Nathaniel Guy.

I am also deeply indebted to Mr. Chas. J. Myers, Ph. C., the genial druggist; Dr. M. A. Majors, author of "Noted Negro Women" and other distinguished works on the Negro race; Mr. George W. Ellis, F. R. G. S., also an author, whose ability already procures him a niche in Who's Who in America; Mr. Richard Westbrooks, partner of Mr. Ellis; Messrs. Preer, Megahy, McMahon, Welsh, Mr. and Mrs. Lane, Mrs. Ida B. Wells Barnett, courageous and persistent agitator for the rights of her sex and her race; and Mr. Terrevous Douglas, President of the Antilia Protective Association.

The volume brought me many pleasant surprises, many encouraging letters from persons I had not known. One of the most agreeable of these letters was from Miss Zonia Baber, Professor of Geography and Geology, University of Chicago. Miss Baber not only commended the work, generously saying that she thought it the best literature she had read on the subject, and that she had placed it on the required reading list for her class, but did me the honor to invite me to represent the African at a Universal Races Congress, in miniature, that she had organized. The Negro, or rather Justice, has friends and stanch friends in many a place one little thinks and Miss Baber, who, I make bold to say, is animated in the highest degree with that spirit of democracy, that catholicity of taste and thought whose increasing influence is today inspiring the world to sublimer, nobler ideals, is certainly one of them. In her letter she told me that for many years she had been striving to erase color prejudice from the minds of such of her students as entertained it. And I must not forget to add that Miss Baber bought, I think, a dozen books, sending them as presents to influential friends in different parts of the country.

I have also to thank Dr. George Burman Foster, Professor of the Philosophy of Religion at the University of Chicago, and Dr. W. N. C. Carlton, Librarian of the Newberry Library. Prof. Foster, in spite of a crowd of pressing duties, read the work in Mss., suggesting helpful improvements, and Dr. Carlton, on receipt of the book, immediately read it and sent me a most appreciative and touching letter, and generously according it a place in his Library. I can not but voice my feeling that Drs. Foster and Carlton represent the beau ideal, the quintessence of that culture, which the noblest minds of the Caucasian race have for the past three thousand years been unweariedly watering and cultivating. I shall be gratefully indebted to the reader to bear in mind that of the many harsh things I found it regretfully necessary to point out about the Caucasian race in this work that I had ever in my mind's eye the exception of this type of which Drs. Foster and Carlton and Miss Baber are so inspiringly representative.

Of the periodicals I must thank Messrs. Talbert and Washington, editor and manager, respectively, of the Pullman Porter's Review. These gentlemen entered heartily into the spirit of my aim even to the extent of offering to and running without charge advertisement in their magazine. Of the newspapers I have quite specially to thank the Indianapolis Freeman for its ample and encouraging review.

I am also grateful to the New York Times and the Brooklyn Eagle for their kindly notice.

And last but by no means least have I to thank my friend F. Leroy Holmes, artist, for the supervision of the printing. Mr. Holmes, I might add, is trying to do for the race with the brush what others are doing with pen and voice.

Again, I thank you all, my friends, I thank you, deeply, cordially, and I assure you that I shall ever fondly treasure your words and smiles of encouragement.

A word or two about the present volume.

This volume is the expansion of a single thought, expressed in "From Superman to Man." The thought, which was expressed for the first time in philosophy, so far as I know, is as follows:

Inasmuch as every civilization the world has known, has gone down or out and that even as the present ones have their rise and adolescence like the others it is safe to assume that they too will decay; therefore it would no more be desirable to have the whole world civilized at one and the same time than it would be to have all the land under cultivation or all the ore in use. Hence, undeveloped peoples should not be despised.

The thought, as I say, may or may not be original, but one thing seems sure: few of the wisest of that most developed variety of the human race sense this fact even subconsciously, or how to explain that race's great disdain for primitive people and the tendency to regard their undevelopment as guilt?

Another fact regarding the volume:

Remembering how books on sex are barred from the mails in the United States—the most cultivated persons will talk sex facts in an indelicate manner but will be quite shocked to see these same facts presented in the coldest manner in print—I thought it wise economy to omit certain data

which I had spent a great deal of time and effort in secur-
ing and which would have given stronger point to my theory
of racial intermixture.

My sole aim has been to express "the truth as Nature
leads." In planning the volume I had in mind the old
Roman engineers who laid out their roads in a straight line,
cutting through all obstacles. Truth is light, and perhaps
the second most remarkable quality of light is the direct-
ness of its rays. There are always two theories of every
subject, one of which contains more truth than the other,
and my aim has been merely to glean from both, using as
my guide experience and an open mind. As everything that
is, is truth, so by truth I mean that principle which at every
present moment upholds the right of the honest individual to
life, liberty, and the pursuit of happiness regardless of
"race" or religious beliefs.

The reading of "From Superman to Man" is essential to
a better understanding of this volume; indeed it would best
precede it.

J. A. ROGERS.

PROLOGUE

I.

Washington, D. C., 1913.

A wave of Jim-crow bills was sweeping the United States. In the legislatures of Wisconsin, Iowa, New York, Minnesota, New Jersey, Michigan, Illinois and Indiana—states hitherto regarded friendly to citizens of African descent— had been introduced anti-marriage bills, and now in the National legislature had been introduced a national bill to prevent mixed marriages.

This eruption of ill-will was due, it was averred, to the marriage of a stenographer of European origin to a noted pugilist of African descent, in spite of the tearful pleadings of her widowed mother, and the hostile rumble of public opinion. This irritation, following sharply the crushing defeat of the white champion by the black one and the consequent heavy financial loss in the defeat of the favorite, it was said, was too much for the whites, and they had urged their representatives, civic, state, and national, through press, letter and telegram, to the introduction of these bills.

The bill had excited a feverish interest at the capital, and for days past had been the leading topic. Numbers of visitors had come from adjacent southern states to hear the debate and to lend their support, and every available seat in the balconies was occupied.

A Southern Congressman, with one eye, but whose burning brilliancy compensated for the loss of the other,—a man of commanding height and a voice that dominated the hall— had taken the floor, and with gesticulation of arms and a terrific smiting of palms was pounding in his convictions with dynamic vigor and intensity.

Gentlemen, he was saying, never since the day that the white man superseded the Indian, never since the day the decision was made that civilization and not barbarism should rule this Western Hemisphere, have we been called to decide a question of graver import. Think well upon what I am going to say. Do you realize what a fearful danger threatens the culture of the western world? Do you realize how the venomous, diseased, jungle blood of Africa like a slow and deadly poison is creeping over your civilization and mine, turning its lily purity into blackness. Forty-two years ago when as a boy I trod the streets of this proud and beautiful city Africans were the color they ought to be, but now you see them of all shades from black to white. As white and as blue-eyed as you and I. But white and blue-eyed only on the outside. Inwards they are as black as midnight in the depths of their native jungles. A man may be as white as the drifted snow on the inaccessible mountain peak, his eye the blue of the skies of sunny Italy, his hair of the finest silk from the loom of the Creator, his nose as perfect as the ravished dream of a sculptor of old Greece, but if one single drop of African blood pulses in his veins he is pure African. No scientist needs determine it. It will be unmistakeably evident in the depravity of his morals and that lack of respect for law and order, that utter lack of virtue and chastity so markedly characteristic of the colored race. (Applause, followed by hisses.)

Gentlemen, the danger lies greatest in that they look like you and me and all the rest of us. But nothing is further from the truth. They are no more like us than midnight is like mid-day. Take a lump of coal, put a beautiful coat of white enamel over it, does it not remain a lump of coal? So it is with the white Negro. The Ethiopian can change his skin but he cannot change his heart. Deck a hog in silk and he will return to wallow in the mire. Two hundred years of civilization and look! They are no higher in virtue and morality than their brothers in the jungles. They have no conception of virtue (applause and hisses). Gentlemen, do not misunderstand me. I have no prejudice against the African. No man is a better friend to those Africans who will stay in the place for which an all-wise Creator intended them, hewers of wood and drawers of water for our race— the superior race. I speak from a sense of duty, the duty I owe my race, the peerless all-conquering Anglo-Saxon. Consider the majestic morality of the white race, its glorious traditions, the inheritance of six thousand years of the

greatest civilization the world has ever known and then bar-
barous, benighted, cannibalistic Africa who, in the same
long span, has accomplished nothing, nothing, absolutely
nothing. I most emphatically insist that the Ethiopian is a
menace to Anglo-Saxon culture. They have not hesitated
to mix shamelessly with the white race and to glory in their
bastardy. They are proud of the blood so shamefully acquired. Let not sentiment deter you any thought of personal liberty. It is only the worst of the two races that
mixes. The white man who will stoop to consort with an
African woman is already of a low type of beast. The white
man who will mate with a black woman, who will so far
debase his body, the temple of the living God, merits the
penalty of this bill. You owe it to your wives, your daughters, your sons, to support this bill to protect them from this
menace. Anyone of these white-skinned blue-eyed Africans,
God perish the thought, may mate with your son, your be-
loved, your cherished daughter, your beautiful white daughter, the pride and darling of your life-long dreams, and produce Oh, horrors of horrors, a child of purest Africa, coal-
black, flat feet, blubber lips, nauseating odor, and woolly
detestable hair. How would you fathers—and you mothers
too, sitting up there—feel to see your daughter standing at
the altar of matrimony beside a black nigger? How would
you feel? How would you feel? The black nigger is nothing but a brute, he is beneath a dog. Think of it and support this bill. This bill should receive the support of every
member of this historic hall, and any white man who has
not sufficient love for his race and honor for its glorious
deathless traditions to support it, is unworthy of the love of
his people, the wife of his bosom, the children of his loins,
his country and the people who honored him with their votes.
He is a traitor, a double-dyed traitor to his race. The question, the burning question is, Shall the Anglo-Saxon maintain his unspotted purity of blood, his matchless integrity,
his refinements, his culture and soar, soar, ever upward,
upward to the stars, the glorious day, or sink a mongrel into
the hideous, hopeless cannibalistic quagmire of African
night? It is impossible to conceive how anyone can hesitate
on such an issue—an issue of such paramount world importance. Like the fearless Joshua of old I stand here and say:

Choose ye this day whom ye will serve: The African or the
Anglo-Saxon, night or day; light or darkness, morality or
hideous immorality. You cannot serve both. If you favor
Africa, you are an enemy of America. As Joshua decided,
"As for me and mine, I will serve the Lord," so I stand here
every nerve, every heart-beat quivering to the thrilling, the
magic word "Anglo-Saxon," and say I stand now, now and
forever for the unsullied purity of the white race, for progress and not darkness, for the Anglo-Saxon and not the African, and I exhort you by the love you bear to your race, by
the duty you owe to your offspring, to the unanimous support
of this bill.

Gasping for breath, the Georgian staggered to his seat
amid a roar of mingled jeers and applause coming from both
sides of the house alike.

And he seemed to have made many converts, to have defi-
nitely fixed the wavering views of many. Many whose better judgment might have prevailed in behalf of justice and
individual freedom were swept into acquiescence by the
dynamic appeal to racial oneness and the effluvium of mob
spirit that pervaded the hall like a subtle penetrating essence. Many members, however, appeared to have taken
no interest in the matter. Upon their faces and in their
postures could be read quiet resignation, while others so
hardened by years of senatorial combat, that their feelings
had become quite leathery, and impervious to sentimental
stimulus of even this sort, appeared to be dozing peacefully
quite oblivious to the startling appeal of the champion of
white supremacy, whose lips dripped venom so fluently.

Among the large number of visitors in the balconies were
the three friends: James Trent, a university student; Robert Hamilton, postoffice clerk-laborer, on a visit to the capital city, and Walter Perry, an artist. Keenly interested in
everything that concerned the welfare of their people, they
had come to hear the debate on the bill.

With increasing bitterness gnawing at his heart, Trent
had listened to the revilement of his people, and now the
applause evoked by the speech whipped him into so wild an
indignation that he could no longer hold himself in check.

"By God," he gurgled, grinding his teeth in rage, "I
would like to put a bullet into his fanatical heart. If I only

had a gun, that damned roughneck—that da-a-a"—and turning to speak to Hamilton on his left, he stopped suddenly, in open-mouthed amaze at what he saw.

Hamilton was among those applauding the speaker!

"Well?" fiercely drawled Trent, when he had recovered his breath.

"Are you crazy?" also demanded Perry, with an angry nudge.

Still Hamilton continued to applaud. When the applause had subsided—Hamilton being one of the last to cease—they both pressed him indignantly for the reason of his evident erratic conduct.

Hamilton, after a reposeful laugh, explained,

"I was applauding old Esop."

"Old Esop?" came the surprised query from both.

"Yes."

"Well?"

"Do you remember that fable of his, where the jackass dressed himself in a lion's hide and went scampering over the fields making a terrible noise and thinking he was roaring like a lion, when all he could ever do was to bray like an ass? Well, that noisy Polyphemus reminded me so irresistibly of that particular jackass that I had to cheer old black Esop for his clever fable."

Perry's response was a sickly half smile.

Trent was unappeased.

"Laugh as you will," he continued petulantly, "I hold that no man with red blood in his veins can sit here and see malicious ignorance stalk naked and unashamed in a place where truth and justice and they only should prevail."

"What he said wasn't true, was it?" inquired Hamilton, in a lazy tone.

"No."

"Well, since it is not true, there is no cause for anger," and then in a cheery, animated tone, at the same time slapping Trent on the shoulder, he continued, "Besides, we colored folks are not the only ones our tactless friend is offending. Didn't you hear him say the white man who consorts with a colored woman is a beast and deserves the penalty of the bill? Rest assured, my dear boy, that many of the applauding ones up here and on the floor would like to wring his neck on the quiet."

"Good," laughed Perry, quite won by this sally. "If the white people can stand for that sort of thing, in this of all places, well let them. They are hurting themselves much more than they are us."

Trent continued to grumble.

"I don't blame you," sympathized Hamilton, "but don't be so impatient. Learn to know that while truth moves slowly it goes in a line mercilessly straight. It is ignorance that always has to do the side-stepping, to make the excuses, to talk extravagantly and with much waving of arms."

"But how are you going to get the truth to them? What are you going to do in a case like this?" asked Trent, with continued irritation.

"Not to adopt impulsive methods, my boy. Fighting fire with fire is bad—in arguments. Cold water's the thing, cold, clear reasoning. Squelch your opponent with a shower of facts. Sh-h, let's listen to this member from Pennsylvania."

The congressman from Pennsylvania, suave and polished, spoke eloquently and warmly in praise of the colored citizen. He drew a touching picture of how the Negro had been brought to the United States against his will, the great suffering he had undergone, how he had fought loyally to uphold the Union, and of the great progress he had made. He then expatiated on personal liberty, and how he thought every one should be free to marry where he wished. The passing of such a law, he concluded in a voice vibrant with righteousness, would be a deadly blow at the spirit of freedom of which America was the world symbol.

And he sat down amid loud and continued applause in which the three friends joined heartily.

"That's better," said Trent, enthusiastically.

"A very good speech," beamed Perry.

"Well, things weren't so black as you thought they were," said Hamilton. "Among every group, however oppressive or unjust, are ever to be found those whose inmost natures revolt at injustice to others, regardless of race or religion, men and women with the cosmic mind, a type which sees in every other human being a replica of itself.

"But," he added thoughtfully, "I cannot share your enthusiasm, at least so far as the nature of the speech is concerned. It was not concrete enough for me. You will notice he did nothing to decisively nullify the impression made by the Georgian—to question his competency to even speak on the subject. This he should have done by the presentment of the facts to prove that so-called intermarriage is not the horror the other pictured it. His speech was merely a matching of sentiment against sentiment, pride of country 'gainst pride of race. The only way to squelch a demagogue is by meeting his glibness and exaggerations with precise and logical reasoning, by pinning him down to facts. Oh! what an opportunity! Ye Gods! I would barter my hope of Elysium for a chance to meet that Georgian face to face in open debate in a place like this."

The house now adjourned and the visitors began to leave, pouring down the steps out into an Indian summer afternoon of beneficent beauty. Perry, appreciatively sniffing the tang of approaching winter in the air, buoyantly suggested a walk home for dinner, to which the other two readily agreed. As they walked the stately avenue they talked.

"The more I think," resumed Hamilton, with conviction, "the surer I am, that if we are to have effective representation, we must make strenuous endeavors to have congressmen of our own people. However good and just a white man may be, I doubt his capability to represent us. He is far more likely than not to lack the experience—our peculiar experience—and so will never be able to uphold our cause as effectively as one of us. Every heart must know best its own troubles. We need colored representatives of a type bold, unafraid, sensible—men who have come in touch with life, men who have studied the situation from all angles and are not afraid to stand up to an audience were its members Olympians and each Olympian no less than the terrible Zeus himself, and tell them the plain, unflinching truth to their faces."

"You already know how deeply I feel on that subject," said Perry, "how heartily I agree with you."

"And not in politics only but in every other field—in literature, art, music," agreed Trent. "Take a book like —— that is attracting such a deal of attention just now. For a Caucasian author, it is of unusual fairness and knowledge

of our living conditions, and while I have no other than
gratitude and commendation for authors like these who have
been so good as to interest themselves in us, yet I do feel
and I regret to say it, there is a something lacking in their
portrayal of our people—the nobler sort, I mean—some interpretation that seems to miss them entirely."

"Lack of experience," said Hamilton. "Anyone who attempts to portray the life of a people in a manner to satisfy its thinking element must live and suffer with it, must
experience all its longing and discontent, must feel the
chafings of the ambitious man who rages at the injustice
which bars him from reaching the place he feels is his, as a
newly-caged lion at the bars between him and his native
liberty, must experience that profound depression arising
from hurts unjustly inflicted, a condition he is impotent to
relieve in spite of all the good he may do, must experience
that indignation which so boils in his breast, that on hearing of some new injustice, however gentle he may be, he
feels like Caligula when he wished that all his enemies had
one neck, so that he could by one swish of the sword be rid
of them forever. To write of a people one must see them
on the heights and in the depths, must feel as they feel, must
live their lives as they live it, in short, must envisage all the
circumstances peculiar to the situation. Expression of ourselves must come from ourselves. And before we can feelingly do so, we have much to unlearn. We must learn to
shun the deadly mechanical and frigid civilization of the
white man as we would a prison—a civilization, whose members conspire to make of one another boxes, and not human
beings—a civilization that would reduce humanity with its
soul-moving variety of tint, color, and shades of feeling to
its own cold, white and sorrowing pattern."

Several steps they walked, each buried in his own thought,
then Perry resumed:

"While we have every opportunity of observing Caucasians in all walks of life, private or public, on the stage,
pictorial or animated, in short, while their life is an almost
open book to us, yet, they, on the other hand, do not really
know us. That many know what is known as the "good
nigger" type is true, and even that knowledge is not only
superficial but egotistic."

"The other night at the club," said Trent, "I heard a visiting editor from the South imitating some Georgia Negroes, and although I do not relish such buffoonery, I was half amused in spite of myself. The stories were of the usual conventional stuff, possum-hunting, chicken-stealing and filthy stories reflecting on the virtue of colored women in general. I, too, feel that any interpretation of our life to fully satisfy, must come from one of us. No Caucasian could have penned 'The Souls of Black Folk.'"

"Why, they never mix socially if at all with the better class of our people. I never see any of them at our balls, parties, or any functions that show the better side of our social life, and how can they?" said Perry. "They have placed a barrier between themselves and us, and then expect to know all about us. They see the humbler element and that, along with the doctrine of our supposed inferiority instilled in their youths, blinds and deafens many. A very large number, too, however inferior, spiritually and intellectually, believe that there is a something inherent in them, something akin to the divine right of kings, which makes them superior. Patriotism, said Dr. Johnson, is the last refuge of a scoundrel; similarly, racial descent is the last refuge of some white rogue, hardly fit to live."

"A feeling of superiority," said Hamilton, "which if manifested by a Chinese, Japanese, or Hindoo, would at once be dubbed racial conceit. In my sleeping car days, I had on one trip a Brahmin lady who kept aloof from the other passengers and was quite cold to their friendly advances. Upon my explaining that she was a Brahmin, and that Brahmins consider themselves superior to other people and that many of them would never mingle with whites, despite social status, were, several of them, loud in condemning her attitude. I did not have the heart to tell them that the Brahmins have an infusion of Negro blood."

"Might not the attitude of our people," said Trent, "we make the crossing here—as I was saying, might not our attitude as a group have something to do with the exaggerated opinion that so many of these persons have of themselves? A very large number of our people unconsciously assume an attitude of inferiority, and are only too ready to play second fiddle even when coercion is absent. This remark I heard the other day is not at all rare, 'Well, I tell you, the Jews are just hangers-on like us, glad to be alive,' or that the United States is a white man's country. Persons who talk and feel like that, are, to my thinking, mere lumps of animated human meat, born to serve their betters."

"A man must believe in himself," agreed Hamilton, "must find his chief value not without, but within, and until he does that, not all the powers of Heaven and earth can help him. Yes, I do fear that many of our better and even of our best colored people have the idea of inferiority so ingrained that, as you .say, they unconsciously assume an attitude of inferiority. One of our most famous Negroes, Dr. J. W. E. Bowen, a Who's Who in America, speaking of the word Negro says, 'Let the Negroes rise up and wipe away the stain from this word.' When has there ever been a stain on it, I would like to know?"

"According to this way of reasoning," interposed Trent with a half laugh, "it is the stolen object and not the thief; it is the kidnapped, and not the kidnapper; it is the Belgians enslaved by Germany's superior force on whom there is a stigma."

"The talk of superiority contributes nothing to my irritation," continued Hamilton. "A man might get on the housetop and trumpet his superiority and my inferiority until from sheer ego he explodes like the frog in the fable, and get only my amused silence for his pains. 'Don't tell me who you are,' says Emerson; 'what you are speaks so loudly, I can't hear you.' This talk of superiority is too noisy to be genuine. Its most ardent supporters have the strongest doubt of its validity." Then as after thought he added, "What does irritate me, though, is the immortal cowardice of the whole thing and the phonographic repetition of noble ideals that goes with it. To me the most detestable of breathing things is a coward, those who take advantage of superior numbers to oppress others. One striking feature of Anglo-Saxon culture is its extreme cowardice. Millions of white men would attack one Negro if it were possible for all of them to reach him at once. History contains two examples of cowardly conduct that will live on forever. Xerxes egging on his army of a million to attack the three hundred Spartans at Thermopylae and the conduct of the powerful

Anglo-Saxon toward a race that has never done him anything else but good. Let's walk through that little park if it isn't out of the way."

"How did the doctrine of Negro inferiority begin, anyway?" asked Trent, as they made their way through the park. "From the dawn of history developed peoples had been living with undeveloped ones and there had been no such doctrine. There has been no doctrine of Indian inferiority, and the Indian, concurrently with the Negro, has been a slave in every part of the New World. A difference of color would furnish no excuse. The ancient Britons were of all shades from black to white, while the Jews were fair and the Egyptians black and brown skinned. While the Romans were the inheritors of five thousand years of human achievement, here were an adjacent people yet cannibals. You can imagine how crude these Celts were, for, when it was proposed to bring numbers of them to work on the streets of Rome, Cicero said emphatically, 'Do not take one of them, they are not fit for use.' "

"As late as the fifth century, A. D., the Anglo-Saxon was a savage," said Perry. "Here is a bit I culled from 'Ancient and Modern Britons,' by David MacRitchie," and stopped to read from the note book:

"Even our far later, Anglo-Saxon progenitor, when he first landed in Britain, was a very fair specimen of an untamed barbarian indeed. He tattooed his face like the esthetic New Zealander; he captured his wife by main force like the unsophisticated Australian, and he lighted the need fire with a wooden drill like the primitive Hindu. It was only at a later date when missionaries from civilized Rome and civilized Ireland, had introduced a little southern and Celtic culture that the gentler Christian Anglo-Saxon took to buying his wife with so many head of cattle like the commercial Zulu, instead of stunning her with a club like the simple minded Australian, and to painting his face in stripes like the intelligent Redskin instead of pricking it with a needle like the amiable Polynesian."

How do you account for the doctrine of inferiority then?" again inquired Trent, as they resumed their walk. "It puzzles me."

"The presence of Christianity," replied Hamilton.

"Christianity?"

"Yes, without Christianity there had been no doctrine of Negro inferiority. This doctrine originated with the Puritans in their attempt to combine greed with the teachings of Christ. The Puritans, as you know, were noted for their squeamish religious conscience. How very ticklish the Puritan conscience was may be judged from the fact that women who became mothers on Sunday were barred from the church and baptism refused the infants. According to Albert Payson Terhune, there was, at a much later date, serious discussion among the churchmen whether Benjamin Franklin who was born on a Sunday should be permitted to receive baptism. Rome, as you said, had no doctrine of inferiority; why? Because the Romans believed that might made right, and frankly lived up to it. There was no doctrine of Indian inferiority because Indian slavery was a physical and financial failure. The value of an Indian slave was much below that of a Negro. Negro slavery paid well and hundreds of millions of dollars were invested, many of the most pious Puritans being share holders. How then to retain Christ, with his doctrine of love and self denial and at the same time, the huge profits from slavery. Why, invent a pedigree for the slave showing he was cursed by God? As any doctrine, however destructive to life and morals, can find indorsement in Holy Writ, the fable of Noah dooming Ham to eternal slavery was fitted in. This theory, for which there is not the slightest foundation, came later to be accepted by the brightest minds, and still seems a matter of common belief among Southern newspaper editors and politicians. In short, the doctrine of inferiority is simply the way to justify greed. But there is now not even this pretext. All that can now be offered is a difference of complexion.'

"Speaking of proving things by the Bible," said Trent, "The West African Negroes made a pedigree for the Caucasian, which, ridiculous as it is, is more plausible than the Ham story. According to them, the mark of Cain is a white skin. Man, they say, was originally black, but when Cain killed Abel, and God shouted at him in the garden, he became so frightened that all his features shrunk, and the black faded from his skin leaving him a deadly white."

"We have permitted the whites to shape things too much

for us," said Perry, "and it is about time we began to sit up and do some thinking for ourselves. Take the term Negro. It is the rare African, who ever hears that term. If we are Afro-American, the so-called white man is Euro-American. He is not a white man because only sunlight is white; not Caucasian because Caucasians are of Mongolian stock; not Anglo-Saxon, because even the England of Edward III, contained few, if any Anglo-Saxons; not an American because the Indian and the Eskimo are the only Americans."

"Here's a great puzzle to me," said Trent. "Why, why is it that Caucasians should mix and persist in mixing with the Negro, in spite of all opposition? From their earliest infancy, they have been taught to hate and despise us and yet they will not leave us alone? Why should they mix? Now, tell me that."

"Nothing to that," said Perry, abruptly, "lust, that's all."

"But my dear boy," objected Hamilton, "your reply leaves us no wiser than before. Why is lust? Why is one woman a demi-monde with no thought for the future of the race, and why a mother, who thinks almost wholly of it? Why is a pander who thinks only of self gratification, and why a genius whose thoughts are focussed on the whole universe? Besides, look at the many kinds of lust—lust after power, wealth, knowledge, God."

Perry answered in detail concluding with, "It's chiefly that, I tell you."

"That is the popular belief," replied Hamilton, "But popular beliefs so nearly always contain more error than truth, that with the exception of two or three of them, we are nearly always safe in rejecting them. Knowledge advances and masses of even the most developed peoples, with their leaders, are always from five hundred to two thousand years behind the most beneficent thought. I know Shufeldt gives that as the cause why sensuous white women, as he calls them, prefer colored men but I must reject that opinion on account of its vulgarity. Looked at comprehensively, it would be a terrible indictment against the fair sex at large.

"The fair sex!" interrupted Perry. "The suspicious sex,

rather. You do not think about women as deeply as I do. Tolstoi with the richness of his experience said, 'All my life, I have been lowering my estimation of women and I find that I have still to lower it.'"

"And why are they suspicious, pray," inquired Hamilton. with emphasis, adding, "I believe that every bad and defamatory thing that Shakespeare, Tolstoi, the Bible, and others have said of women is true of the majority, but it is equally true that for every bad trait in woman there is a corresponding one in man. Woman has a bad name in literature, because it has been man's sphere. Many of the bad qualities in woman are often directly awakened by men. And worse, some of the most detestable things that have been said of women are also true of most politicians, not a few newspaper editors, and of groups of humanity, especially the most advanced groups of the so-called Caucasian race. I shall be glad to discuss this later, but for the present, I wish to refute your statement about lust. If it is, as you say, how do you account for the union of the white man and the black woman, which is far more frequent. One thing is sure: Nature has a just and sufficient reason for everything she does, and if pre-conceived notions prevent us finding it out, it is our fault, not hers. Consider the thyroid gland. Because it is ductless the scientists for a long time thought it superfluous and useless, but now it is known to be one of the most important of the glandular bodies, since it exercises a profound influence upon growth and mentality. Nature, as I say, has a just and sufficient reason for everything. Everything that happens, happens with the strictest necessity, and if ever there was an affair of Nature it is this mixing of black and white. Please do not think I am scolding but the truth is that a very large number of persons of even the best type entirely lose their heads in discussing what they call miscegenation.

He paused, then added whimsically, "But I have not a word against those who scold Nature or make statutes to annul her laws. Serves Nature right, I say. Who was it that endowed such persons with that grade of intellect?"

"Don't blame Nature," said Trent, "She gave brains to these persons as she gave sharp-rending tooth and claw to the lion, or to the pig a snout, a means for making a living and not for the solving of social problems."

"And are they not using it as the pig, his snout," returned Hamilton. "Color prejudice persists because it pays. Is not color prejudice the meal-ticket of a writer like Thomas Dixon?—Dixon whose bread is soggy with the blood of creatures he so affects to despise. As long as certain real-estate agents, employers of labor, newspaper men, politicians, motion picture magnates can eat, wear, marry and reproduce their kind off this injustice, so long will it persist. It is men like Senators Hardwick, Hoke Smith, and John Sharp Williams, and States like Florida and Georgia, with their huge profits from convict labor that are the Negro problem, and not the Negro."

Their arrival at home now ended the conversation, but Hamilton while arranging his toilet for dinner, continued to reflect on the question posed by Trent.

Yes, why should the Caucasian seek a union with the Negro, when there were such very good reasons that he should not, he cogitated. No other group of people in the world had ever been so cruelly misrepresented. From the Negro's earliest entry in America, everything that the mind could suggest had been brought forward to be-little him. He was "a beastly creature without God, law, religion or commonwealth; he was a relic of the pre-Adamite period, having neither part nor lot with the human race; the beast spoken of in the Bible; a cross between a male Caucasian and a gorilla; the serpent that tempted Eve; he was degenerate, thievish, lying, murderous, presumptuous, lascivious, malodorous, and God knows what else besides, yet these same contemners did not hesitate to enter into the most intimate of human relationships with this despised people, and even against the will of the contemned; many of the best and choicest spirits preferring these despised women to their own highly cultured ones; men like Clay, Franklin, Jefferson, having colored affinities; Negro hating demagogues pausing between yelps to rear a parti-colored brood, and after nearly three hundred years of this abuse and revilement unparalleled in history this mixing was still going on. Ought it not to be clear to even the most club-footed intellect that Nature was striving to say something?

"What was it?"

The train of reflection caused the fact of Negro-Caucasian intermixing to visualize itself with startling distincness and he was suddenly seized with a great urge to reason it out.

II

Shortly after this incident, Hamilton returned to Chicago, and at once began to gather all the information from books and from individuals that he could. So engrossed was he with the topic that whenever not over fatigued by his work at the post office, his brain would at once revert to the reason for racial intermixture. After a great deal of thought, and combating of counter-theories he had at last formulated a theory. This, from time to time, he resolved to write out in order to more clearly understand, possibly to even publish but on each occasion the stimulus necessary would not flow to his pen. He might have continued thus indefinitely had not the following letter from Trent whipped him into action:

My Dear Hamilton, it read, do you remember that conversation we had some three years ago about the blending of Negro and Caucasian? Well, the thought has kept teasing me from time to time, but my studies have prevented my devoting any time toward reasoning it out. At last, however, I have a theory, which, although I find distasteful, appears so like the truth that I fear I will have to accept it.

This theory, though, is not mine, but that of a white professor of sociology.

I will tell you how I got it from him. The other night while waiting on him at the club where I work after classes he engaged me in conversation. I soon found he is writing a book about us, and of course I became at once very much interested. We talked a great deal then, and two nights past while waiting on him again, I took occasion to ask him the above-mentioned question. His reply is the enclosure you will find.

Perry and several others, including some of my professors, are also inclined to accept it as the truth, although, like me, they do not like it. I also find support in "The

Negro Year Book." In looking it over, I saw this confirming statement: "The tendency as reported," says the author, "is for the Negro race in Brazil to marry up instead of down, that is, there is a tendency for the blacks to marry mulattoes, and for the mulattoes to marry white." Knowing that you are a hard thinker, I am most anxious to know what you think of it. Perry, and all the boys send their most cordial greetings.

Opening the typewritten enclosure, Hamilton read:

THE THEORY OF MISCEGENATION.

The mixing of Caucasian with Negro is merely the second stage of that evolution of progress which began with protozoa and ended in man, for even as there are two stages in the evolution of a stalk of corn, one to the time when it flowers and ceases to grow and another from the blossoming to the ripening of the ear, so there has been two stages in the evolution of man—one, the growth from ape-man through troglodyte or cave-man up to savage, and the other from savage, with his narrow racial outlook, up to the gentleman with his universatility of taste and thought. Like the stalk of the corn the former evolution of man, has ceased, the latter is now taking place.

This progress from savage to gentleman is accomplished by two methods: education and racial assimilation. The mixing of Caucasian with Negro is the latter form of evolution.

The most convincing proof that this theory is the correct one is the manner in which the mixing is taking place. Cold-bloodedly scientific as it may sound, for Nature knows neither ethical nor sexual morality, what do we find? We find this mixing is taking place between the males of the more developed race, and the females of the less developed. Now man represents a higher grade of intellectual and physical development than does woman. With the mixing thus arranged we see that the higher development of the male flows toward the less developed race and nothing from the lower race toward the higher. The Negro race is elevated without lowering the standard of the Caucasian. Should these people become one following the historical precedent, the gain of the whole human race is evident. On the other hand, the mating of the man of the less developed race with woman, the weaker of the sexes, will not only not tend to elevate the human race, but if the woman be of the higher race, there will be that much development lost. Intermixture between Negro and Caucasian is merely Nature's way of raising the Negro to a higher level.

Two distinguished sociologists, Sir Sidney Olivier and Lester F. Ward, support this theory.

In "White Capital and Colored Labor," Sir Sidney says: "There is a good biological reason for this distinction. Whatever the potentialities of the African stock as a vehicle for human manifestations and I myself believe them to be like those of the Russian people exceedingly important and valuable.....the white races are now in fact by far the further advanced in effectual human development and it would be expedient on this account alone that their maternity should be economized to the utmost. A woman may be the mother of a limited number of children, and our notion of the number advisable is contracting, and it is bad natural economy and our instinct very potently opposes it to breed backward from her."

For Lester F. Ward's opinion read, pages 358-360, of his Pure Sociology, beginning with, "We have seen at a certain stage."

Hamilton took down his copy of "Pure Sociology," and having found the place read:

"We have seen at a certain stage, rape was a form of marriage, and that it was based on the unconscious but universal sense of the advantage of crossing strains which is re-enforced by the charm of sexual novelty, both of which motives are equally products of the biological imperative. It will be interesting to trace the influence of these early principles into later stages of society where rape has become a crime. The philosophy of rape as an ethnological phenomenon may be briefly summed up under the following heads:

1. The women of any race will freely accept the men of a race which they regard as higher than their own.

2. The women of any race will vehemently reject the men of a race which they regard as lower than their own.

3. The men of any race will greatly prefer the women of a race which they regard higher than their own.

These are fundamental and universal principles of ethnology and when closely analyzed will be seen to be all the result of the more general principle which makes for race improvement. When a woman of an inferior race yields to a man of a superior race, there is a subconscious motive, probably more powerful than physical passion, which is indeed the inspirer of the physical passion itself—the command of nature to elevate her race. When a woman of a superior race rejects and spurns the man of an inferior race, it is from a profound though unreasoned feeling that to accept him would do something more than to disgrace her, that it would to that extent lower the race to which she belongs. And when the man of an inferior race strives to perpetuate his existence through a woman of a superior race it is something more than mere bestial lust that drives him to such a dangerous act. It is the same unheard but imperious voice of Nature commanding him at the risk of "Lynch Law," to raise his race to a little higher level.

In this last case, therefore, the philosophical student of races, however much he may deplore anything that tends to lower a higher race sees reason for partially excusing the crime since although the perpetrator does not know it, it is committed in a large measure under the influence of the biological imperative. It may be compared to the brave conduct of the male mantis, or male spider in his zeal to perpetuate his race. On the other hand, the indignation and fury of the community in which such an act is performed is to be excused in a measure for the same reason. Although the enraged citizens who pursue, capture, and lynch the offender do not know any more than their victim that they are impelled to do so by the biological law of race preservation, still it is this unconscious imperative far more than the sense of outraged decency that impels them to the performance of a much greater and more savage "crime," than the poor wretch has committed.

The terrible penalty attached to this attempt to raise

a lower race by lowering a higher one, renders this form of race mixture very rare. Fortunately, for the human species at large there is a fourth law, which may be stated as follows:

4. The men of any race, in default of women of a higher race, will be content with women of a lower race.

The necessary corollary to all these laws is that in the mixture of races the fathers of the mixed race almost always belongs to the higher and the mothers to the lower component race. What the effect of this is upon mankind at large is matter for speculation. Whether the opposite would produce a better or poorer mixture is not known. That it would be a different one there is little matter for doubt, the difference might be compared to that between a mule and a hinny. At all events the process of race mixture that has always gone on and is still going on through the union of men of superior with women of inferior races is at least in the nature of a leveling up and not a leveling down."

Hamilton replied that same evening as follows:

My Dear Trent: As you may imagine, I read your letter and its accompanying theory of racial intermixture with the keenest interest. You ask me what I think of it? Well I shall relate an incident that flashed through my mind even while I was reading it.

Two young fellows with no experience in mining went in the California desert in search of gold. After many days of weary fruitless search, and the enduring of great hardships they at last saw a huge rock which fairly glittered with yellow metal. Overjoyed, and with visions of ease and a competency for the rest of their lives they loaded themselves with the glittering specimens and trudged the long way home cheerily. Arriving at the city, they went straight to the registry bureau, filed their claims and thence to the assayer's office. The assayer took their ore, and after breaking it up gravely inquired their story. When he had heard it all, he said sympathetically: "Well, fellows, I am very sorry for you, for this that you believe to be gold is a very inferior metal, called iron pyrites or fool's gold. I am very sorry for you and the only consolation I can offer you is that even experienced miners are sometimes deceived by it."

Affectionate regards for self and all the boys.

Very truly yours,

ROBERT HAMILTON

A few days later came a post-card saying:

My Dear Hamilton: I told the sociologist what you said of his theory. He was very much struck and I fear not a little hurt by your comparing it to iron pyrites. He is most anxious and so am I to hear your theory. Won't you send it at once?

Hoping that you will be able to successfully disprove him.

I. A. TRENT.

A week later, Hamilton replied:

I take great pleasure in forwarding my theory or rather its first installment. My inability for sending it entire is due to two reasons: My desire to go into the matter as thoroughly as I can, proving each point as I go; and my having to work at night. I shall endeavor, though, to send you at least a letter each week until finished. Any criticisms from you or anyone to whom you might show them will be most welcome.

END OF PROLOGUE.

LETTER I

My Dear Trent: I must first of all point out that the sociologist has raised another and most interesting query. This is, which is superior: a mulatto whose father is white or one whose father is black, equivalent to saying that the former product tends to leveling up while the latter to leveling down.

To begin, I think it well that we should establish a common basis of agreement and would suggest the following:

It is agreed that black and white are mixing.

It is agreed that there must be a just and sufficient cause for it, since nothing happens without a cause.

It is agreed that intermixture can have but one of two results: either it is to the benefit of the blacks such as the sociologist has given; or of the whites.

With these as a basis we intend to investigate the following:

Why black and white mix.

Which, if any, of the two kinds of mulatto is superior.

My theory, I find, resolves itself into four parts.

1. (a) The attitude of the native African toward a union with the Caucasian.

(b) The attitude of the Caucasian toward a union with the African, native or exotic.

2. The esthetics of color.

3. Predominant Negro characteristics, physical, spiritual and intellectual.

4. The purpose and function of sex.

The first, because it is necessary to determine which of the two sides desires intermarriage the stronger.

The second, to investigate the value that lies in color, in and of itself, since so much stress is laid upon it by the mass of whites and Negroes, cultured and uncultured, alike.

The third, because these are the qualities transmitted

by intermixture. It is not necessary to go into Caucasian characteristics since the sociologist acknowledges that that race is an evolution of the primitive type.

The fourth, because sex is the medium of intermixture. In my next letter I shall discuss the first half of part 1.

R. H.

PART ONE.

LETTER II

My Dear Trent: In my last I promised to speak on the attitude of the native African toward a union with the Caucasian.

In considering this, I invite your attention to a number of observations from some of the best recognized of the African travellers:

Dan Crawford, the missionary who lived for twenty-two years without a break among the Negroes of Central Africa says in "Thinking Black:"

"Unlike the Saxons, Danes and Jutes who were invited by the ancient Britons to enter England, here you have the black-but-comely African honestly warning you off both his soil and his soul. Frankly saying in so many looks if not so many words, that he would rather have your room than your company."

Dr. Mojola Agbebi in his address before the Universal Races Congress, "No un-Europeanized native of Tropical Africa seeks inter-marriage with white people. Commercial intercourse and other unavoidable contact with white people may lead to a progeny of mixed blood but no Tropical African, pure and simple, is inclined to marry a European or appreciate mixed marriages.

The fad of segregation in social gatherings and religious worship recently brought into prominence by the imprudent and impolitic among white people is not distasteful to the un-Europeanized African. The Architect of the Universe has originally determined the bounds of the habitation of every race of man. The African has not overstepped these bounds to seek fellowship, social, religious or otherwise with white people. It is a matter of ridicule to the African therefore that white people should not only trespass into Africa, but come there to propound the doctrine of segregation which Nature has all along placed boundless seas and countless barriers to indicate.

The unsophisticated African entertains an aversion to white people, and when on accidentally or unexpectedly meeting a white man he turns or takes to his heels it is because he believes in the evil eye, and that an aquiline nose, scant lips, and cat-like eyes afflict him. The Yoruba word for a European means a peeled man, and to many an African the white man exudes some odor not agreeable to his olfactory nerves.

Moreover, Europeans are regarded as plague carriers The plagues hitherto known to the people of Tropical Africa are very few, and are subject to already known treatments; but the advent of an influx of Europeans is regarded with evil foreboding by a great many owing to the plagues and diseases that follow in their wake and to which Africans are strangers. Witness bubonic plague, syphilis, cholera and others."

Frances Hoggan, M. D., of London, at the Universal Races Congress: "In the out-lying districts of Africa where Native life is seen at its crudest. white women have no fear, and they pass freely in and out among the Native population, safe and unarmed, never dreaming of danger."

Du Chaillu in his African Adventures:

"It is curious that nothing excites so much terror in an interior African village as the appearance of a white man . . . . The women and children run for their lives and seem to be afraid that the mere sight of a white man will kill them."

Rev. R. R. McBriar, M. A. "The African at Home." (A Shuwa girl speaking to a white man.) "We have no fears now; we know you are good, and our eyes which before could not look on you, now search you always. They bade us beware of you at first, for you were bad, very bad, but we know better now. How it pains us, you are so white!"

(I had a white woman, apparently well-educated to remark similarly to me one day on the train. She said after

I had talked with her some time, "What a pity you are colored.")

McBriar: "We have said that the color and religion of a Christian are great scarecrows for the people of Africa."

Darwin: Descent of Man; "The Negroes rallied Mungo Park on the whiteness of his skin and the prominences of his nose, both of which they considered as unsightly and unnatural conformations. . . . The African Moors also knitted their brows and seemed to shudder at the whiteness of his skin. On the eastern coast the Negro boys when they saw Burton exclaimed: "Look at the white man! Does he not look like a white ape?" . . . .

One of the titles of the Zulu King is "You are black."

Mr. Reade does not think it probable that Negroes would ever prefer the most beautiful European women on the mere grounds of physical admiration to a good looking Negress. . . .

Mr. Winwood Reade held that the ideas of beauty of the native African is, on the whole, the same as ours."

Sir Harry Johnston: "Negro in the New World." "There is, I am convinced, a deliberate tendency in the Southern States to exaggerate the desire of the Negro for a sexual union with white women. A few exceptional Negroes in West and South Africa and in America are attracted towards a white woman but almost invariably for honest and pure minded reasons, because of some intellectual affinity or sympathy. The mass of the race if left free to choose would prefer to mate with women of its own type. When cases have occurred in the history of South Africa, Southwest, East and Central Africa of some great Negro uprising and the wives and daughters of officials, missionaries and settlers have been temporarily at the mercy or a Negro army or in the power of a Negro chief, how extremely rare are the proved cases of any sexual abuse arising from this circumstance. How infinitely rarer than the prostitution of Negro women following on some great conquest of the white or their black and yellow allies . . . . the Negro has either had too great a sense of decency or too little liking for the white woman, (I believe it the former rather than the latter,) to outrage the unhappy white women and girls. He may have dashed out the brains of the white babies against a stone, have even possibly killed their mothers, or taken them and the unmarried girls as hostages into the harem of a chief (where no attempt whatever had been made on their virtue), but in the history of the various Kaffir Wars, it is remarkable how in the majority of cases the wives and daughters of the British, the Boers, the Germans, after the slaughter of their male relations were sent back unharmed to white territory."

Dudley Kidd: "Savage Childhood."

"There is, of course, the primitive and initial dislike of a difference of color. Kafir children think a white skin very ugly, and sometimes even revolting. When a very small black child shakes hand with a white man, it instinctively looks at its hand to see whether the "white" has come off and soiled its black hand; it seems very surprised when it finds that the color doesn't come off."

Winwood Reade: "Savage Africa."

"The ladies (of the Fan Tribe), wished it to be clearly understood that they did not object to a fragment of goat skin, a couple of plantain leaves or anything in reason, but they thought it very foolish of me to hide my skin. Was I ashamed of it, because I was not black?"

Alexander Davis: "The Native Problem."

"The tribes of the Zulu stock in their pristine state regard with horror any contact with a white skin."

I could quote many others, but I think one may safely conclude that the African does not wish a union with the Caucasian .

In my next, I will treat the second half of part 1.

R. H.

LETTER III

My Dear Trent: With regard to the attitude of the Caucasian for a union with the Negro, I shall again let the Caucasian speak for himself.

Richard Hildreth: "Archie, a White Slave," (a record of slavery in America:)

"There is a soft winning, captivating way about some of these (colored) girls, that makes them perfectly irresistible. I don't wonder at the envy, rage and jealousy of our white women, they can't help being conscious of their inferiority in this respect. Of course it makes them cross and fractious —natural enough, but that does not help the matter, nor render them any the more agreeable. So they have to be content with being mistress of the house and the servants while some slave girl, black, yellow, or white as the case may be, is mistress of their husband's affections."

(And very often these slave girls paid dearly for this "affection." This instance related by Sir H. H. Johnston, was not unusual:

A Dutch woman in South America, remarking the sweet engaging countenance and remarkably fine figure of a newly arrived Negro girl burnt the girl's cheeks, mouth, and forehead with a red hot iron, and cut her tendon Achilles, leaving her a cripple for life.)

Sir H. H. Johnston: "Negro in the New World."

"The Dutch women had often good cause for jealousy because their husbands after a short residence in Guiana preferred the society of quadroons, mulattoes, and even Indians."

Medical Review of Reviews, July, 1916:

"Before the Emancipation Proclamation, the Southern gentleman came into intimate contact with the Negress. As a baby, he nursed at the bosom of the black mammy, and when he grew up he had intercourse with these women. It

mattered not whether she was of tender years or already
a wife or mother. Whenever he met one of his bond-women
in the fields or in a cabin, if he wanted her, she was forced
to submit . . . .

Physicians think they make a case against the Negro
when they bewail the fact that colored prostitutes are a drain
on the finances of the Southern white man. The white man's
desire for the colored woman has long impressed visitors to
America."

(The reason why Negro troops were barred from George
V's coronation was, I understand, the attention paid by
white women to the Negroes who attended Edward VII's
coronation. One Negro athlete of herculean build and
strength, who won the champion shot-put of the British
Army, beating the white champion by six feet, was a favorite

In the garrison town of Port Royal, Jamaica, the wives
of several of the English soldiers stationed there had affinities among the colored troops.)

Carolyn Wilson, in Chicago Tribune, January 24, 1915:
(writing from Paris.)

"Across the aisle at one of the big reserved tables sits a
blacker than the ace of spades Sengalese. Nearly every
woman in the room is breaking her neck to see him and
smile at him and recently he held a little reception of seven
of the most wonderfully gowned svelte women in the room,
who wished to inquire if he had been wounded or reforme.

It is simply amazing, and to an American revolting to a
degree, to see the attention these men receive. At
the Comedie Francaise, two in a box were the object of all
opera glasses, women threw them flowers, and the entire
audience went into such shrieks of laughter over the remark of one of them that it was necessary for M. Mounet
to stop speaking."

Charles N. Wheeler, Chicago Tribune, Nov. 15, 1918,
says in speaking of the reception accorded our colored soldiers in France:

"In one respect, France is the paradise of the black man.
The social line is not drawn here as at home, owing to the
fact that the French women share their admiration with
the dark-skinned French troops from the colonies."

Iwan Bloch: "Sexual Life of Our Time:"

"White men from very early times have had a peculiar weakness for Negresses and mulatto girls and women. As early as the eighteenth century, there existed in Paris, Negro brothels and somewhat later after Napoleon's Egyptian expedition Negroes and Negresses came in large numbers to Paris, and were utilized for the gratification of the lust of both sexes. Notwithstanding the deeply-rooted racial hatred even in America, racial fetichism gives rise to numerous connections of this kind.

The European newspapers are full of interesting reports of the powerful attractive force exercised by exotic individuals, male or female, such as Negroes, Arabs, Abyssinians, Moors, Indians, Japanese, upon European men and women respectively. Whenever members of such races come to stay in any European capital we hear of remarkable love affairs between the white girls and these strangers.

The colored girl exercises a powerful attractive force upon the American man and even the proud American woman manifests a certain preference for the male Negro with an especial frequency in Chicago. But much greater is the alluring force exercised by the white upon the black."

R. H.

LETTER IV.

My Dear Trent: In your last letter I see that the sociologist wishes to know how I can reconcile that last sentence of Bloch's: "But much greater is the alluring force exercised by the white upon the black," with what I had already said about the Negro's attitude toward the white woman. As you will recall, I spoke of the native African. Bloch's statement concerns the exotic, so I think it would be well to examine the attitude of the exotic Negro toward a union with the Caucasian.

Before doing so, however, I should like to call the attention of the sociologist to this fact: Not only has the white man an affinity with Africans, but Africa also.

Mary Gaunt: "Alone in West Africa," says:

"Africa holds. The man who has once known Africa, longs for her. In the sordid city's streets he remembers the might and loneliness of her forests, by the rippling brooks he remembers the wide rivers rushing tumultuous to the sea, in the night when the rain is on the roof plashing drearily, he remembers the gorgeous tropical nights, the sky of velvet far away, the stars like points of gold, the warm moonlight that with its deeper shadows made a fairer world. Even the languor and the heat he longs for, the white foam of the surf on the yellow sand of the beaches, the thick jungle growth densely-matted, rankly-luxuriant pulsating with the irrepressible life of the tropics. All other places are tame. The fascination that he has denied comes back calling to him in after years. Thus the whirligig of time brings in his revenge. This mistress he will have none of has spoiled him for all else . . . . Africa holds, and the man she holds may yield to the fascination, not only without shame but with pride."

Ernest Morgan: "Around the World."

"The word Africa still conjures up visions of wild

animals, black people, and burning sunshine; of phlegmatic Boers, Congo Slaves, and Belgian "atrocities," in general, of a good place to stay away from. Many wonder why nations should fight over it, and why men who come away seem smitten with a mad desire to get back again. For nothing is truer than that the Africander, of whatever race, or nation cannot get the Dark Continent, out of his heart and brain." R. H.

LETTER V.

My Dear Trent: In my last letter I promised to write of the attitude of the exotic Negro toward a union with the Caucasian. I think we can find no better key to its investigation than the four laws of racial inter-mixture given by Lester F. Ward, and quoted by the sociologist. Their discussion will, I am sure, not only help to answer his question, but also give us an opportunity to see how true these laws are in regard to the Negro.

1. The women of any race will freely accept the men of a race which they regard as higher than their own.

I will also ask you to consider concurrently another social law which I will as broadly state.

The women of any social status, regardless of race, will freely accept the men of a social status which they regard as higher than their own.

As you know, in all countries, savage or civilized, but more so in highly civilized ones, wealth and social position are powerful factors in a woman's final choice of lover or husband. Women, at a very early age, begin building castles in the air about their marriage. If poor, they look forward to having a rich husband, able to take care of them and their offspring. Then, too, money means the maintenance and quest of beauty, as seen in the care of the body or in personal adornment. This is especially true of cities or social centers, where the competition of woman against woman is very keen, especially in the case of women who possess beauty, and those not so well favored. Love of adornment is woman's great weakness, and this is justly so, since her passive role makes this form of appeal necessary for her chief goal—masculine appreciation, a husband. Incidentally, it also gives her one of her keenest delights, making other women jealous. The thoughts of the average woman centres in her physical appearance and since mas-

culine appreciation is her goal, she reads the measure of
her value in her power to attract the male. The stirring
picture drawn by Shakespeare in Richard III, where that
grotesque monarch won Anne, who a moment before had wished him in hell for the butchery of
her husband and her father-in-law, by telling her that it
was her beauty that had provoked him to the deed is no
libel on the sex. That woman's ego should lie in her appearance is not derogatory to the sex. Not only is there
a male equivalent—the dandy, the man who powders and
primps and who feels his hold on life is slipping when
women no longer gaze on him in public places, but it is
quite natural. Life is first physical, then spiritual, then in-
tellectual.It is the rare man who does not find his chief attraction for woman in her physique. Therefore it is to the
interest of woman to at all times present her best appearance. Masculine appreciation is to woman what water is
to the thirsty plant, the pole to the tender vine, the sun
to the earth. Just as the devotee feels happiest when he
makes a complete surrender to his God, whatever it may be,
money, intellect or a mental idol, even so is a woman most
blissfully happy when she surrenders herself on the bosom
of her lover. The stronger the personality of the man, the
less inclined will he be to surrender to any god. The stronger the personality of the woman, the less inclined to surrender to any man. This, I think, is the principal reason
why well-educated women and women of forceful person-
alities are less likely to get married than others, and not
that usually given that men do not like educated women,
but which is of course true of women possessing only bar-
ren intellectuality. The woman of education and personality, especially the latter, demands higher values and weak-
minded men are usually afraid of this type. It takes worth
to appreciate worth.

A strong factor in marriage, was, as I said, social position. For social conquest is to women what conquest in
war, or achievement in art or commerce is to man. In
Europe, the beautiful and untitled girl, rich or poor, if ambitious, often dreams of marrying a lord. Sir H. H. Johnston tells of the craze of certain English girls to marry

Zulu princes or Ashanti noblemen. The daughters of the lord if ambitious, looks forward to marrying the son of a duke, and that of a duke, the son of a king. The daughter of a kinglet, say of one of the many little German kingdoms, looks forward to marrying the son of a leading monarch. In America, the ambitious girl itches to get into "society" and if in "society" often wishes to marry a duke or count. Titles, as has been so well depicted by Edmond About, in "La Mere de la Marquise," have a powerful attraction on the ambitious girl, regardless of race or nationality. So, too, does any other kind of distinction as in the arts, letters or even pugilism.

And what is true of women is also true of men. The newly rich in America or elsewhere will make every effort, pay large sums to enter what is known as exclusive social circles. There are, I believe, few dyed in the wool American democrats, however much they might turn up their noses at titles or decorations, who do not feel a certain elevation, when in the company of a foreign nobleman. The desire for distinction of some sort—something to mark one as being different from the other fellow—is firmly imbedded in human nature. From time to time one hears of foreign impostors bamboozling American plutocrats. Recently, a French cook, Edward Rousselot, posing as a marquis, had the cream of the "society" of New York and Washington, at his feet. Thackeray, in "Vanity Fair," has ably depicted this craving of the untitled to enter titled society. The truth is, that people of certain social orders are always trying to get into a social order they consider higher than their own. Now what titles and social positions are in Europe—the standard of social values irrespective of mental or moral worth,—the lord may be a diseased rogue, and yet be considered the superior of an honest, healthy, and intelligent commoner—even so is a white, or more properly, an almost colorless skin, a standard of social value in America, so far as "race" is concerned. As rank in Europe means enlarged opportunities, so does a near colorless skin in America. As in Europe, the commoner is taught even from his infancy, to look up to a lord so in the New World, and especially in the United States, the so-called Negro has been taught to look up to the so-called white man, in short, "white" ideas predominate, as in Europe titular ones do. In Europe few noblemen there are who would not feel displeased if mistaken for a commoner, and few commoners in Europe or America who would not feel pleased if mistaken for a lord. Again, in the household few mistresses there are, who do not feel insulted when mistaken for the maid—a reason why many white women prefer colored maids—and few maids who would not be reciprocally pleased. Similarly, in America, few whites there are who would not feel insulted if mistaken for one of Negro descent. It is libel to call a white man a Negro in Louisiana, South Carolina and Georgia, and he may recover damages. On the other hand, there are few of colored descent who would not feel it highly pleasing if mistaken for white. In Europe the man who lives well, lives like a lord; in America, like a "white man." In Europe if he works hard he toils like a peasant; in America like a "nigger." This also finds expression among the colored people. Not infrequently a colored man who earns, say forty dollars a week, will boast that he has a "white man's job," mindless of the fact that the wages of the average white are much below that figure, and that the United States, with the highest paid workers, contain but a small portion of the so-called white race. The influence of all this upon the mind, or rather lack of mind in the female, makes her look up to the white man.

But to pursue my comparison. Just as in Europe certain commoners wish to enter lordly society, and those in that society are doing their best to keep them out, because they believe them inferior; just as certain newly-rich in the United States are doing their best to enter certain circles, and the members of these circles are doing their best to keep them out, because they believe them inferior, just so are certain Negroes doing their best—though in an indirect manner—to enter white society, and those in that society are anxious to keep them out, as they too, believe or pretend to believe them inferior. It is in this sense that I agree to Ward's first factor in racial intermixture. We see though that false values can be set above real values—that a diseased lord may be ranked higher than a worthy commoner, that in America a diseased social parasite may be ranked higher than an honest, healthy and intelligent workman, that a white criminal may be ranked higher than a healthy intelligent colored man, in short, that a social value is not necessarily a biological or natural one, and that values created by the intellect of man, may be in direct opposition, to those values, conducive to the health and happiness of the human race. My deduction, therefore, is, that there is no difference between the feelings of a girl who surrenders herself to one she believes of a higher social order whether that status be titular, professional, or pugilistic and that of a girl, say a Negro, who surrenders herself to one of a race, she has been taught to believe superior. It is one and the same case of love dazzled by distinction.

I believe that most colored women, the ambitious ones of course, would prefer a white man as a husband or lover. This would no doubt be generally denied in the United States by colored women, but it is true of the British West Indies, where the weakness of the color bar permits mixed marriage and there is nothing to prove that there is any fundamental difference between the woman of mixed and unmixed descent of the United States and her of the West Indies— indeed that there is any well-defined mental or spiritual difference between women of widely different varieties of the human race. Women are much more similar in their nature than are men. Their minds run chiefly to things sexual—love-making, care of the home and children, and dress. I have listened to the conversation of women of all classes and it is mostly chatter of these things. As I say, it is my opinion that the colored girls of mixed and unmixed African descent wherever found, whenever they come into social contact with the whites, would, consciously or unconsciously, prefer a white man on account of the higher social value, and the better advantages to their offspring. Not a few colored women believe that in order for a child to be of consequence, it must be light-skinned and flossy-haired. I heard a full-blood African street preacher once tell a man of similar extraction, "Anytime a woman of your color has a child for you, she sure does love you." And I recognized its truth so far as the Negro woman of the social centres are concerned.

I will conclude the discussion of Ward's first factor in my next letter.   R. H.

LETTER VI.

My Dear Trent:

In your last letter, I see that Perry objected to my saying that colored girls would sooner marry white men, offering as a rebuttal that a very large number of our light-skinned girls marry men much darker than themselves. I reply that here we have again to deal with that important characteristic of the female mind—the desire for masculine appreciation. In the West Indies where the color bar is weak and where "light" girls are free to marry white men, they rarely, if ever, marry men darker than themselves. Rich, colored girls will often prefer a poor white man of the better class, even as the rich American girl will often prefer a poor nobleman. In the United States, "light" girls will marry dark men. As we saw the color popularly known as white is a standard of social value. Now certain black men, feeling the great handicap of color, desire to identify themselves with white or as near white as they can, as also desiring to give their children a better start than they had themselves seek the "lightest" woman they can get, and in order to get her are willing to give more value, that is, more appreciation in the way of admiration, gifts and other attentions dear to a woman's heart, than a light-complexioned man would be inclined to give. I have this direct from the lips of these women themselves. One of these girls told me that there is hardly anything a black man would not do for one of her kind. Another girl who is almost white, and whose husband is dark, tells me that she was prompted to marry him, although she did not really love him, because he was so attentive. She said, "Kindness goes a far way towards winning a woman."

I here crave permission to digress long enough to make certain observations I consider highly pertinent to the racial situation.

Although this attitude of certain black men is most detrimental to that bold, magnificent manliness, already so lacking in the Negro, since success of this sort, indeed success of any sort with women, means the suicide of a man's better self on account of the great amount of deception necessary, yet, there is more good than harm for the future of the race in this his desire to get "light" women. It effectively prevents a third or mulatto caste, such as exists in the West Indies. To have us so divided is just what the whites want, and many white scholars are now attempting it. The Negro who draws color distinctions within his own group plays into the hands of the whites and is his own worst enemy. The whites say that anyone with a drop of Negro blood is a Negro. The most practical thing for us to do is to accept that dictum, and if we do, they are going some day to most heartily rue it.

And yet another thought: the effect of this kind of marriage on the light woman?

It is not only responsible for many of these women being so spoilt, and becoming so conscious of their looks as to render them quite unfit for serious thought, but also for wifely infidelity, for nothing—gifts, honor, all—can deceive love very long. The same holds true of white women married for social position and not love. Even as the beautiful woman among the whites is much more likely to be lower in morals than the plain one, on account of the incessant attentions of men, so I believe the light-colored girl represents a lower moral plane than either the black or the white one. Indeed, this is actually so, except among the better families, where wholesome training intervenes; light-skinned girls of large social centers are, with the exceptions just mentioned, not of very high worth, morally. Courted assiduously by black, white, and parti-colored men they not infrequently become the wife of the first and the paramour of the others.

To resume the highway of my discussion: I see the sociologist asks of the attitude of the light-colored man toward a union with the black woman. I do not think the light-colored man is inclined to marry the black or rather dark women, but masculine vanity plays its part here. Most men are egotistical in marital affairs, and the dark woman is more likely to idolize her "lighter" husband—to make a greater to do over him. One fact I have noticed is that the number of male parasites is much larger among light-skinned men than dark, and that their prey is usually a woman darker than themselves. Rascals, whose only claim to distinction is the squalid one of brightness of skin and slickness of hair, will have some black woman wearing herself out to keep him loafing.

In closing this letter, I will add my concluding thought to Ward's first factor in racial intermixture: It is evident that the desire of certain colored women to marry white men, and of certain black women to marry mulatto men, like that of certain white women to marry titled foreigners, is artificial, rather than natural. "Woman," says Weininger, "seeks to create as much personal value as possible for herself and so adheres to the man who can give her the most of it"—a fact independent of "race." The value may take the form of flattery, intellectual or physical accomplishment, and wealth or social position. This, of course, does not include the woman of personality, she who is sure of herself, and does not shine with borrowed light.

LETTER VII.

My Dear Trent:

Ward's second factor of racial intermixture, as I promised. "The women of a superior race will vehemently reject the men of a race they regard lower than their own."

As you know, the vogue in this matter of mixing is for the Caucasian to hold himself an irresponsible minor. Be there an intimacy between a white man and a colored woman, it is the woman to blame; be there one between a white woman and a colored man, it is the man to blame. Some years ago at a meeting of the National Association for the Advancement of Colored People, a gentleman from Virginia suggested as the best means of solving our color farce, the leaving alone of white men by colored women,—Aesop's fable of the wolf accusing the lamb, who was drinking below him, of muddying the stream. There is also the Jack Johnson incident. The impression the newspapers gave to the world was that Johnson was running after white women, while the truth was that he had to do far more running from, than at, them. White women, good, bad, and indifferent, used to pester him often out of all patience.

There is a tendency on the part of a very good many to regard as depravity all liaisons or friendships between white women and anyone not belonging to the so-called Caucasion race. Especially is this the case when the so-called Negro is in question. White agents and others who visit the homes of colored men with white wives seem to think that any kind of conduct goes. White men who have colored affinities, and consider it quite natural, think the union of the colored man and white woman sacreligious. This, too, is the attitude of nearly every American writer and the majority of English ones.

But I fail to see why this should be so. I have given a great deal of thought to the subject, having lived with such couples in the United States, Canada, and in the West Indies, and can find nothing approaching the unnatural or depraved but this: Throughout the animal and vegetable world, it is the male, who, except in rarest instances, goes in search of the female. In the United States, however, it is the white woman who nearly always makes the advances to the male Negro. As an illiterate janitor in his crude way said to me in relating his amours, "You must wait till they ask you or they will holler rape." This, too, is independent of the double dealing that such meetings often entail. In the West Indies there is nothing of this sort, except in the case of the foreign white women who have colored affinities. White women of the upper classes not infrequently marry colored men. I know three brothers all married to white women of most respectable families. One of these, the daughter of a wealthy Scotch clergyman, has reared a family of fourteen children in a refinement whose delicacy and charm is equal to that of a European of the best class.

Liaisons between white women and colored men began with the entry of the Negro in the New World, and in spite of the severest penalties have persisted. Today they are frequent with the women, as I said, nearly always taking the initiative, except in the case of these white women in houses of assignation, and even then it is they who took the first step by going to these places. A Southern white girl told me rather positively that she believed the majority of Southern girls had colored lovers. How true this is, I do not know. Several instances, private and public, have come to my notice though, and I have heard of the relations that existed between the slaves and certain of their mistresses, during the Civil War, while the white men were at the front. But even the racial hostility that exists in the South is no proof that Southern white women have no liking for Negroes, or to be more precise, certain Negroes. Just as in the case of the West Indian girls and the colored American ones there is nothing to prove any fundamental difference between the white woman of the South and her of the North. And the number of so-called white women of the North who have, or have had colored affinities, and those desirous of meeting them, I have cause to believe is very large. Moreover, as we saw, the white women in Europe seem to like colored men, and I do not think even the racial dogmatist will attempt to prove any fundamental difference between the white women of Europe and those of America.

But the most convincing proof that many white women in the United States have an unconscious liking for Negroes, that they would never acknowledge perhaps even to themselves, is the vehemence in that rejection of which speaks Lester F. Ward. Now, in order for these women to vehemently reject Negroes, they must have been thinking deeply about a union with Negroes, and why think about a union with Negroes if they have no liking for them? Peter's vehement denial of Christ was due to the fact that he had had affinity with Christ. When the Empress Josephine was accused of illicit relations with the gigantic Negro who used to bathe and dress her, did she fuss and storm? No, she merely laughed and had the man married to one of her women. The case of the white woman who vehemently protests against the suggestion of a union with Negroes and that of the woman-hater is identical. The woman-hater has a strong dislike for women, but in spite of himself, he is attracted to certain women, nay, bound to women by ties, few women-haters are powerful enough to break, and so, by violence of language against women tries to deceive himself. Similarly the white woman who violently rejects Negroes has a dislike for Negroes, but from time to time she meets certain Negroes who appeal irresistibly to her, and is angry at the thought that they should. In Europe, this woman would give play to her feelings, but in America she must conform with environment, and so to kill self, she storms at the Negro just as Aesop's fox abused the grapes he would gladly have eaten. Many white women object to sitting beside a Negro, however handsome and refined because the close contact lowers their powers of resistance. On the whole, I must agree with Bloch that the white woman has a liking for individual Negroes. I shall confirm this later on by showing that the principle of attraction operates the same in both sexes of the Caucasian race.

I could tell of the hundreds of these meetings in high and in low life that have come to my notice, of heart stories that are waiting for an American Maupassant, and will briefly

relate one or two in order to reveal, as I hope, more clearly
the psychology of color prejudice:

One day some colored men were passing the windows of
a corset factory in Chicago. Some white girls seeing them
called to them and began to flirt, dropping, before the men
left, slips bearing Christian names and telephone addresses.

One of these men in talking with a friend of mine, I will
call Jones, told him of the incident. Jones, who is ever on
the qui vive for adventures of this sort, asked for one of the
addresses, and getting it, he called on the telephone. The
answering voice, a feminine one, said that the person called
was out. Jones, who is a great man for picking acquaint-
ances over the phone, at once started a conversation. Now
Jones has unusual success with women. Not only is he well
built, having once been an athlete of international reputation
and of decidedly distinguished appearance, but he is extraor-
dinarily fluent. Even as Nature gave the spider a web for
enmeshing flies, so she gave to Jones a mellifluent tongue for
trapping women. Jones is endowed with an abundance of
that small talk so essential for success with women, and I
have heard him talk with them over the phone for perhaps not
less than an hour at a time on silly nothings. Jones, too, unlike most men, in talking with women, concentrates the conversation on the woman, saying just enough about himself to
pique their curiosity. He now opened this honeyed battery,
and the delighted girl, at the close of a long talk, asked him
to call again. Among other things he learnt that she was a
university student. The next day he called again, and soon
she wanted to meet him. Jones objected that she might not
wish to meet him as he was a Brazilian and rather dark. If
Jones has ever been to Brazil, it must have been that in Indiana. Jones then learnt that she had a violent antipathy for
Negroes, why it was she did not know, but she hated them,
and would never sit by one in a car—but, of course, according
to American notions, Africans from Brazil and the West
Indies are not Negroes, only those of the United States are.

But Jones had so impressed her that she wished to meet
him, and suggested that he appear at a certain place where
she could see him unknown and then judge of his color
whether she would like a closer acquaintance. But Jones
indignantly refused, telling her that if she wished to see

him, he would either come to her place or she must come to his, and hung up abruptly. She immediately rang again and after the necessary persuasion decided to visit Jones at his place of business, saying that she was going to have her brother accompany her. The brother did not come with her, anyway. Whatever might have been her feelings toward Jones' color, they at once became fast friends. Jones is rather dark and bears unmistakeable evidence of his African ancestry in features and hair. From time to time she would utter her great dislike for Negroes, which made Jones secretly angry.

One day a poet of some distinction, and about Jones' complexion, visited the place while she was there, and was, with her spoken consent, introduced. When he was gone, she became very angry and scolded Jones. "The idea," she stormed, "of your introducing me to a 'nigger'. The next thing you know he will be seeing me on the street and speaking to me."

Well, their friendship continued, she thinking that Jones was going to marry her. That she had doubts of his ancestry was evident, because she would often study his complexion and hair, and one day after such study, she remarked: "Dear, I always thought my Prince Charming was going to be so different from you."

Now Jones, as I must tell you, is already married. Married to a white woman, who makes him a most excellent wife, and lives only for him. She is a "typical" wife, she believes in her husband and whatever he does is right for her. They had lived as neighbors when children and had grown up loving each other. The parents objected most strenuously to their marriage. Jones, though, despite his escapades, is of better social calibre than his wife and her parents.

Jones is very skilful at his business, and when I first met him, he was earning eighty dollars a week or more at a down-town place, working part time, and was saving his money to go to live in Europe, where he has twice been in an athletic capacity and as a student. In spite of his escapades Jones is devoted to his wife and had no intention of deserting her.

As this girl, the university girl, was apparently well bred, and of no inconsiderable degree of personality, Jones hesitated to approach her indelicately. One day, though, he did, making some rather forward advances, and she dashed out of the office in a terrible rage. Jones was very much frightened, fearing that she had gone to tell her brother. He now determined to have no more to do with her, but, to his great surprise, she called him again in a few days, and soon after recommenced her visits. He approached her once more and this time she conquered him with tears.

Jones now determined to break off all relations with her and gave out that he was going to Lower California, not knowing when he would return. She cried heartily. She soon found out he had not left the city, and began to call him again. She would call at nights, and when the answering voice was not Jones', she would hang up without answering. The person who lived in the rear of the office complained of this to Jones, and he, upon tracing it, found it came from this girl, who used to work as a telephone operator at nights. Anyway, they met again, and she would visit his place of business, always holding out for marriage.

About this time Jones became interested in a Mexican colonization scheme floated by a white man and he had this white man to confirm to her what he had said about his being a Brazilian and also to tell her that he was doing this man's translating. Jones knows a word or two of Spanish, which he mispronounces, and not a word of Portuguese. I must not forget to add that this white man, also married, asked Jones, from time to time, to introduce him to colored women. Seeing how blindly the girl had fallen in love with him, Jones determined to take a step that he hoped would end all. He confessed he was already married. There was a terrible scene. She wept till her heart was like to burst, and declared that her faith in men had been shattered forever. It was her first love. As a last resort he offered the grim consolation of his ancestry, saying that she would not have had him even had he been single. But the shaft of love had sunk too deeply and now race, color, nothing, mattered. It was human heart seeking human heart. She pleaded with him to give up his wife, saying that she would have to make as great a sacrifice in giving up her parents and friends, and one day in despair she went with her bank book to where he worked down-town, and showing it to him, offered to pay all expenses of elopement.

And now comes the most interesting part. Some time after, Jones introduced her to his wife, and she made friends with her and the baby. She took an interest in the poet, even doing some typewriting for him. Her antipathy for Negroes as a race is quite gone. In a recent letter to Jones, she wrote this enchanting bit: "I shall never forget the feeling of repulsion I had on entering your—— nor how quickly it vanished after I had talked with you. After a while the place breathed Romance, and I would not have exchanged it for all the tapestried, Persian-rugged palaces in all the world. My imaginative soul transformed your faded rug into a woven miracle fit for the feet of kings, and your dilapidated furniture into rare antiques."

But her lesson was a hard one. Jones, who now appreciates her fine spirit, has since expressed his keen regrets for the incident, although he is also of opinion that she deserved her lesson for the way she used to talk about "niggers." Had he known she was that kind of girl, he would have acted differently, he says, as he realizes how indelible the effect of such incidents on a woman's life.

I know of similar incidents, though not so tragic. Persons, however prejudiced, can never tell what they are likely to do. Propinquity and personality are more than a match for prejudice. Prejudiced persons are often so because they have never been able to see clearly, and if they ever do, like Saul of Damascus, they usually endeavor to do all they can to make reparation. A converted Negro-hater is usually the warmest champion of Negroes.

This story, which is scrupulously exact, and a great deal of which came under my direct observation, proves, by the way, what I have just said about vehement rejection of Negroes by white women.

A great deal of prejudice is, too, a mere blind. Just as the Prussian soldier stiffens himself the minute he sees an officer, and from a smiling human being becomes an automaton ready to obey any command, so do many white associates of Negroes when the sight of another white person recalls the sway of the King of American democracy. This is especially true of women. Byron's statement about women being taught to deceive is especially applicable to white women. Yet, they are much better at heart than the men, for while white men take their colored sweethearts into alleys and dark streets, such as I have seen, and friends of mine who collect the night mail tell me, the white woman, if she loves the man, will boldly appear in public.

The discussion of this second factor of Ward's will be continued in my next. R. H.

LETTER VIII.

My Dear Trent:

Do you remember my saying in the last letter that vehemence of rejection instead of being an expression of dislike might proceed from the opposite? Well, I have since found what I consider striking confirmation of this theory in "Miscegenation," a work by a Caucasian author of slavery times and one who seems to know what he is talking about. In the chapter "Heart-Histories of the White Daughters of the South," he says:

"Nor are the Southern women indifferent to the strange magnetism of association with a tropical race. Far otherwise. The mothers and daughters of the aristocratic slave holders are thrilled with a strange delight by daily contact with their dusky male servitors. These relations, though intimate and full of a rare charm to the passionate and impressible daughters of the South, seldom, if ever, pass beyond the bounds of propriety. A platonic love, a union of sympathies, emotions, and thoughts, may be the sweetness and grace of a woman's life, and without any formal human tie, may make her thoroughly happy.

And this is the secret of the strange infatuation of the Southern woman with the hideous barbarism of slavery. Freedom she knows, would separate her forever from the colored man while slavery retains him by her side. It is idle for the Southern woman to deny it; she loves the black man, and the raiment she clothes herself with is to please him. . . .

Passionate, full of sensibility, without the cold prudence of her Northern sister, who can wonder at the wild dreams of love which fire the hearts and fill the imagination of the impressible Southern maiden? . . .

It is safe to say that the first heart-experiences of nearly every Southern maiden, the flowering sweetness and grace of her young life, is associated with a sad dream of some bondman lover. He may have been the waiter, or coachman, or the bright yellow lad who assisted the overseer; but to her a hero, blazing with all the splendours of imperial manhood. She treasures the looks from those dark eyes which made her pulses bound; every spot of earth where he had awaited her coming is, to her, holy ground.

The first bitter lesson of a woman's life—self-sacrifice—they learn when prejudice and pride of caste compel them to tear the loved image from their hearts. What wondrous romances are yet to be written on this sad, but charming theme, what wealth of passional life is lost with all the heart-histories of the South blotted out by a blighting prejudice, a cruel pride of caste and colour. The full mystery of sex, the sweet, wild dream of a perfect love, which will embrace all that is fervid and emotional in humanity, can never be generally known until men and women are free to form unions with their opposites in colour and race. The rule in love affinities is the same as in electrical affinities, unlike attract; like repel."

To resume the thread of my last letter.

The volume of intimacy that goes on between colored and white in cities like Boston, Chicago and New York is enormous. If these mixed couples were all to appear on the streets, not only would people soon stop gaping, but the divorce courts would be busy for a long time. Colored women kept in fine flats by white men. Colored men kept by white women, the hardest work many of these parasites doing is to carry around the shoes on their feet.

Mixed couples meet anywhere from a hotel to a closed taxicab. In Chicago, white girls from the North Side of the city come to the South Side, and the sable Haroun-Al-Raschid can always meet many such. When these girls meet colored men they sometimes introduce their friends. And it is a mistake to imagine that these are girls of the street. Many of them have had a desire to meet colored men for a long time, and there is an extra joy, cordiality and good feeling when they do. In many of the larger cities there are places where white women of the better class meet colored men. The keeper of one of these places said to me with a gleam of plantation cunning in his eye, "The white man has the best of our women, and why should we not have some of his?" The go-betweens, I might add, are whites.

I know of several instances of colored men of the better class marrying white women of a similar class. The number of such marriages is much more than white writers would have us believe. The number of mixed marriages in a city like Chicago, principally among the lower classes, runs into the hundreds. The majority of the intercourse of the better classes of both groups is derogatory.

I have no doubt whatever that a very large number of white women, perhaps the larger number, would object to any intimacy with colored men, on account of lack of contact, lower social position, and training. But, as I said, propinquity and personality are powerful factors. Love is no respecter of color, creed, clan, or of biological value as laid down by certain Caucasian writers.

After several years of observation, mainly in the Northern and Western states, there is evident to me a deep, persistent desire on the part of no small number of white persons of both sexes, high and low, to mingle their blood with that of the African. "Africa holds," says Mary Gaunt. And so does the African. White men and women who have once associated with Africans are hardly ever content with their own again.

With this letter I conclude my thoughts on Ward's second law.   R. H.

LETTER IX.

My Dear Trent:

We'll now consider Ward's third law. "The men of any race will greatly prefer the women of a race which they regard as higher than their own."

As we saw the native African has little or no taste for the society of white women. The same cannot be said of the African who comes into long contact with them. One day in a restaurant in Chicago, I overheard a colored veteran of the Spanish-American War deploring to a colored waitress that no colored Red Cross nurses were being taken to France to care for the colored soldiers. The waitress listened with an ominous calm, and then said with a flash of scorn, "Now don't tell me that. White women like colored men as much as they do white ones, and if you would rather have a colored woman to wait on you than a white one, believe me, you are an exception." His companion, also a veteran, retorted, "I'll tell you why. When we were in a hospital, the white woman would come around with an apple, an orange, or a flower, while the colored woman would come around with blood in her eye, thinking somebody was trying to take away her man." In spite of this excuse, I thought the waitress the winner of the tilt.

On another occasion, while speaking with a distinguished Negro author, he said, "We do not extend our dislike for the race to the women, we leave that to our women." The truth is the men of opposing groups are not, as a rule, ill-disposed toward the women of the other group. The dislike is strongest between the same sexes in the two groups. In attacks on tribes or nations in olden times, the women were often spared. The Jews, in spite of their racial egotism and religious hostility, used to bring home the virgins while they relentlessly butchered the older women, the men, and the children.

I spoke of the native African having no taste for the society of white women. This is, to a great extent, also true of the African in the West Indies. In the West Indies there is practically no evident desire on the part of the black or colored men to meet white women. I attribute this to the fact that while color has a strong social value there yet it is a weak factor in economic advancement. There, as in Europe, freedom from earning one's living is considered a mark of gentility. Colored men can, as a rule, get almost any position for which they are fit, and there are no laws or strong conventions to prevent them from marrying white women. Again, nearly all the whites and near whites are proprietary, and of the better class, while the majority of the blacks are of the peasantry. There is also hardly any desire on the part of the blacks to marry mulattoes, as is the case in the United States. On the whole, I think the well-marked class distinctions which nearly always places one, regardless of color, in the place he belongs, is the strongest factor in the preservation of color harmony south of the Rio Grande. The color question in the West Indies is not a pressing one. Color topics are not frequent, while in the United States they have a foremost place among Negroes and the whites of the South. In the British West Indies, the chief topics are the glories of the British Empire and religion.

In the mountains of Manchester, Jamaica, live a considerable number of whites of no higher social status than the colored people. They go barefooted the same as the blacks, and there is little or no attempt on the part of the black man to marry these women. The colored peasantry are inclined to look down upon them, calling them "White labor," in contrast to the "Buckra" or proprietary class.

But what I have said of the West African and West Indian Negro is not true of the American one, or of the West Indian in the United States. There are, I think, three causes for this.

First: The large number of whites of no higher social status or capability than an equally large or larger number of Negroes.

Second: The United States is supposed to be a democracy where all men are equal.

Third: The advertisement given by anti-marriage laws and conventions:

Now this actual and this supposed equality in conjunction with the restraining influence of the third enhances the value of the white women in his eyes.   We generally believe that which is out of our immediate reach better than that we have.   Eve might not have touched the apple if Jehovah had not called her attention to it by interdiction.   We are forever reaching at something and when that is attained at something else.   Life is a continual striving.   White is identified with better advantages, hence, many ambitious Negroes want white, often placing on it, as I shall late prove, a value out of all proportion.   However, when such Negroes marry white or near white they are merely trying to attain that color which the white man says they must reach in order to get their rights as men and citizens.

Mere curiosity is also a powerful factor and prompts many colored men to seek the association of white women. On the occasion of Negro excursions to Chicago, white demi-monde   reap   a   rich   harvest.   Mere   curiosity   also prompts many white women to seek the company of colored men.   Similarly white men who go South from states like Nebraska and Minnesota, where colored women are scarce, look forward to meeting them, and sometimes ask train porters to direct them.   A European friend tells me that when he decided to come to America he looked expectantly to meeting a colored woman and how much disappointed he was when he saw what conditions were.   He married a white woman, but has had many colored affinities, and quite lost his heart to one.   He tells me that were his wife to die he would marry a colored woman in spite of all.   White women, he says, are too cold, and he doesn't see how anyone can want them when there are colored ones.

On the other hand, I know many Negroes who do not like white women and the great masses in the rural districts of the South, it is safe to say, simply never think about them. In a large city on the Pacific coast, I went to what is known as a "Mannasseh" ball, that is, a dance where the men are colored and the women white.   The girls, mostly waitresses and shop-girls, were fairly attractive.   All but three or four of the men seemed to be enjoying themselves and I heard the patroness, a full-blooded Negro woman, ask one of them why he did not dance. He replied that he did not like white women. "Give me my own color," he said.

"God bless you, honey," was her heartfelt response.

R. H.

LETTER X.

My Dear Trent:

"Do I not think that the Negro in his heart of hearts prefers the white woman?" I notice your sociologist friend has asked.

As you know, the greater part of the conversation of the human race, savage or civilized, black or white, yellow or red, drifts to sex affairs. Men talk about women and women of hardly anything else but men. I have listened to hundreds of conversations by white men, of all walks of life, on sleeping cars and other places, and they nearly always at some stage of the conversation turn to the topic of women—either experiences or stories. Similarly, I have listened to hundreds of conversations of colored men,—porters, professional men and others—and they speak most often by far of brown-skinned—seal skin brown, next of high brown, high yellow and then of white. I think the majority of Negroes prefer their own women, first, because it is most natural with them—white as we see being an acquired taste; second, the coolness caused by prejudice; and third, the uncertainty of meeting these women.

In making advances to white women, most colored Americans are timid, almost cowed. An acquaintance who was approached by a white woman in San Antonio, Texas, tells me he could feel the cold sweat coming out all over his body like moisture on a thawed-out window in the winter. In the Northern states this fear takes loss of position and dread of public sentiment, as well as fear of ostracism of many of their people when they have a white wife or a sweetheart. Negroes have nothing near the boldness of whites. White women are much bolder than colored ones, and many do not hesitate in the least to make their wishes known.

Some white women flirt with Negroes merely to test out or to cultivate their powers of attraction, preparatory to tackling bigger game, and the men sometimes mistake these as well as mere courtesies for the desire to be friendly.

This, however, holds true of men in general. Men not infrequently mistake a woman's frankness for something not intended.

Not a few white women believe that any colored man would be glad to get them solely on account of color. Such are mistaken. I think few Negroes would say of their women what the German gentleman mentioned by Shufeldt said of white ones—that he preferred a black woman to any white women.

One day on the sleeping-car, I overheard a white woman telling some passengers that while she would marry a Chinese, Japanese or Indian she would never marry a Negro. She was past the marrying age, and as I observed her rather crabbed and discouraged features, I could not help thinking that she would indeed be lucky to get any kind of man.

The number of white women with whom many colored men would do no more than exchange the ordinary courtesies is probably as large in proportion as the number that would reject them.

Perhaps my statement that the Negro on the whole prefers his own might also find confirmation in the fact that white women who have colored husbands or affinities are very jealous of colored women, giving a colored woman as the reason at the first sign of coolness in the man. Many instances have come to my notice of colored men leaving white women for their own, while the whites who come among the colored usually stay there.

A taste for the society of white women by Negroes is acquired, therefore Bloch's statement, "But much greater is the alluring force exercised by the white upon the black," is not logical.

But Bloch's statement might be tenable in two cases—that of certain educated Negroes and the rapist. Let us examine these.

There is no doubt whatever that the particular and early training of some Negroes calls for that daintiness, that feminine delicacy best represented by certain white women. They read of the snow-white skin, raven tresses, and flowing flaxen hair of the romantic authors like Scott and Lytton, and this leaves an impression they have never been able to efface, the more so if they have been reared among whites. Such almost invariably prefer white companionship. They are, in short, the product of their environment. Not infrequently these persons have to associate with whites of a low type, even as the whites very often have to take Negroes below them, which is one abnormality of the situation. It happens, not infrequently, that the Negro with which a white woman associates is below her, since, as I said, the white woman nearly always makes the advances, and very few women, however bold, will directly court a man who is a personality, fearing a refusal, which would be a deadly blow to her pride. The white man is also having more and more to take the colored women of a lower class, since the better class are increasing in what is popularly known as race pride.

To settle this question of the educated Negro, I will again compare the liking of the Negro men for white women with that of white men for Negro women.

One evening, while in a cabaret in Chicago, three white men of the better class were seated by the waiter at my table. We soon began to converse. After a short while they asked me to take them where they could meet some colored women, promising to reciprocate. I denied knowing such a place, but they would not believe me, and to get rid of them, I promised I would do so the next evening. If I am to judge by their anticipatory remarks, I should say they were very keen to meet colored women. This cabaret enjoyed unusual prosperity. A newspaper in its crusade against cabarets advertised that there was no color line. Crowds of whites used to visit it, standing in line to get in, especially on Saturday nights. Many of them of both sexes came to meet colored persons, as I learnt from the manager, the waiters and the singers.

Some years ago a Harvard professor was sued in Boston for breach of promise by his colored mistress, a woman of the lower classes.

Shufeldt in his book, "The Negro," says ,"In conversation with a very intelligent German gentleman the other day, a man of fine education, intelligence and family connection in Germany where he was born, he informed me that he very much preferred congress with a fine, good-looking black

Negress than with any white woman he had ever known, and from all accounts he had not been backward in such matters."

This statement, true of a large number of white men, controverts those white authors who maintain that the white man's seeking of the colored woman is mere lust and has no significance. If mere lust and not color—race, was the principal motive, these men could find any number of white girls and, perhaps, with less trouble. Now, when we remember that a sexual union, as so well demonstrated by Schopenhauer, is preponderantly the motive of love, and that a man's association with a woman when it has naught of sex in it, differs little, if any, from masculine association, it is evident that the color lure is the thing, and that, were there no color line, such white men would marry refined black women in preference to refined white ones. One thing may be regarded as sure: when a white man has a white wife, and a Negro sweetheart he prefers the latter, even as the morganatic wife of a king is the real love.

It may be that the difficulty often experienced in meeting the better class of white women might enhance the attraction for certain colored men, but when one considers that the black man has been taught to look up to the white, while the white has been taught to look down upon and even to abhor black, we may safely dismiss Bloch's statement and say that the attractive force of the Negro on the Caucasian is much stronger than the attractive force of Caucasian on the Negro, even in the type of the educated Negro referred to.

In my next I will speak of the rapist. R. H.

LETTER XI.

My Dear Trent:

In my last letter I promised to speak of the rapist.

Here we have these two factors: First, as we saw the native African, even when he had white women in his power, returned them unharmed; second, this kind of attack is peculiar to the United States. In the British West Indies and Hayti, where black outnumbers white; in Cuba, Porto Rico, and Brazil, where white outnumbers black, this condition is practically unknown. Sir Sidney Olivier, in "White Capital and Colored Labor," says, "In the British West Indies, assaults by black or colored men on white women are practically altogether unknown. No apprehension of them whatever troubles society. I say this as an administrator familiar with the judicial statistics. . . . Whatever may be the cause it is the indisputable fact that Jamaica or any other West Indian Island is as safe for white women to go about in, if not safer, than any other European country with which I am acquainted. . . . If, then, there is special ground for fearing assaults of this character by colored on white in America, it clearly cannot be due to any necessary or special propensity of race."

Sir H. H. Johnston, speaking of this passage, says: "The statement may be applied with equal truth to all parts of Negro Africa."

Sir H. H. Johnston further says:

"I was informed by every resident or official whom I questioned that cases of Negro assaults on white women were practically unknown in Cuba. . . .

"It is scarcely too sweeping an assertion to say that there has been no case in Jamaica or other British West Indies, of rape or indecent assault or annoyance (to a white woman) since the Emancipation Proclamation."

Why should this condition be confined to the United States? is the natural question.

Two causes: The reaction of segregation (already dealt with in letter IX), with its desire for revenge and its accomplishment by Negroes chiefly of defective mentality; and merely incidental as when a feeble-minded Negro gets into lonely association with a white woman, when it would have been the same had she been colored. This last might also be true of normal men, under stress of rare circumstances.

What we call defective mentality is the chief cause of rape. It is the impulse of most healthy men to wish to capture the woman, to seize her bodily, and that of the women to be so taken. But training, evolution, restrains this instinct. The rapist, like the shouting, shrieking, religious enthusiast, is merely a helpless instrument in the grip of a blind impulse.

In the list of mental defectives must be included the man who takes drugs or so drinks to excess that he will attack others or attempt to ravish.

Another important consideration. Black rape is exaggerated. White women are often frightened in advance by hearing of Negro rapists, so extensively advertised by the yellow press, in which must be included all but a few newspapers. Ray Stannard Baker has cited several instances in his "Following the Color Line." There is no doubt whatever that many innocent Negroes have been lynched on this account. Some lonely white woman will see a Negro and at once the thought of the rapist strikes her. She screams. The Negro is caught and at once she will say he tried to attack her. Hot irons are applied to the Negro's body, and to gain a temporary respite from death, he confesses. Most women and especially highly nervous ones have a hazy conception of truth. Women live so much in the realms of fancy, always building castles in the air, coupled with the fact that from their earliest infancy they have always had to act a part, make them not infrequently unable to distinguish truth from error and one runs into the other. The literature of all ages and of all climes is full of this weakness of woman, and justly so. As a boy, I knew an elderly lady, a most seeming devout Christian, and the facility with which she could tell untruths to visitors amazed me. Woman's nature runs to sexuality, not intellectuality, and anyone who has considered the psychology of sex will note how erratic, how spasmodic and contradictory is this principle of Nature.

Again, suppressed sexuality often makes women believe they are being pursued by men. Spinsters in delirium generally rave that men are watching them. Cases of rape on grown women should be thoroughly investigated. Herodotus, who apparently had some chance of studying this, tells us that if women do not want to be carried off, it is a hard matter to do so. I read of a man being accused of this crime. The judge was dubious and ordered the accused to give the woman a piece of money, then to follow her and take it away. But she fought so stubbornly that the man could not get it, whereupon the judge dismissed the case.

Again, some of these attacks have been invited. It is well said that if Joseph had surrendered to the wiles of Potiphar's wife and been caught, she could easily have made a case against him. As it was, she succeeded in getting him into prison.

Having considered the cases of the educated Negro and the rapist, we may say in conclusion that Ward's third law,— "The men of any race will greatly prefer the women of a race which they regard as higher than their own," is not valid. That the Negro, as a mass, does regard the white as superior is true.

On the other hand, we find that a very large number of white men, even while regarding their women as superior, greatly prefer Negro women.

In my next letter I will consider Ward's fourth law.

R. H.

LETTER XII.

My Dear Trent:

Ward says: "The men of any race in default of women of a higher race will be content with women of a lower race."

As I have already shown, this would not be true, that is, if I construe it rightly. I take it to mean that Negro men are satisfied with their own women because they cannot get white ones.

Moreover, upon closer examination this statement will be found to be quite meaningless, for not only would the men of any race in default of women of a higher race, be glad to get women of any race, but the women of a so-called higher race, in default of men of their own race, would be glad to get men of any race. It is a certainty that if there were no white men, white women would be glad to get men of any race. As it is many of them certainly prefer men of other races. At eighteen, women are finicky in their choice of men; at twenty-five, they are far less particular, and from thirty-five onwards often glad to get any man who is half-decent; for man is to woman, what the bony frame work is to the body. As the body would be a shapeless, meaningless mass without the skeleton, so the spirit of women is chaotic, fretful, nervous, puling, discontented, without the spirit of man. As Byron says:

"Man's love is of man's life a thing apart,
'Tis woman's whole existence."

On the other hand, even as the flesh lends grace and harmony to the body, rounding out the ugly corners so does the spirit of woman beautify the spirit of man. Woman is man's supreme delight, a joy without which wealth, honor, glory, God, are at times tasteless baubles to the sternest.

That Byron is right in saying that woman's desire for man is greater than the opposite is proved by the fact that woman's share in the reproductive functions is very much greater than man's. The desire for fatherhood is almost nothing as compared with that for motherhood.

In countries where women are in the majority it is the men who are pampered, flattered, and fought over, as in India and England. In regions where men are the majority, it is the women, as in Alaska and mining settlements. (1).

That Ward's fourth law is meaningless so far as it affects our question, is, I think, clear.

And now, having considered these four laws of racial intermixture, I approach the end of the first division of my theory, the object of which, as you will recall, was to determine which side desired intermarriage the stronger, There are, however, a few deductions yet to be made and these I reserve for another letter.   R. H.

* * *

APPENDIX.

(1) This is the sure reason why women are so much better treated, or rather, have more sway in the United States than in Europe, and not that. usually given that American men are politest to women.

If they are, (I shall prove that they are not) it is the shortage of women that makes or made them so. And probably the inspiration for padded shoulders, analagous to false hips in women.

According to the census of 1910, there were six per cent more white men than women, the Negro having two per cent more women than men. This smaller percentage of women no doubt, accounts for the spoilt nature of so many white women, who want not only the rights and privileges of men, but the concessions and attentions usually accorded women. This probably accounts, too, for the mooney, love-sick, crawling way, I so frequently noticed among white men when I worked on the railroad, such reminding me irresistibly of this passage from "The Shaving of Shagpat."

> "Exquisite lady! name the smart,
>   That fills thy heart,
> Thou art the foot, and I the worm,
>   Prescribe the Term."

This exhibition of unmanliness; this sign of fading
virility reaches its most ridiculous form in that masochism
popularly known as Southern Chivalry, and its most perverted and pernicious form in Chicago where it is impossible to get a jury to convict other than Negro women for
the most cold-blooded murder of men. We even find a
certain judge advising a woman to kill her husband.

One thing is sure, the American attitude is not due to respect for womanhood. A man's true character is manifest
not in how he treats women of his class or race, but in his
attitude to all women. The colored woman represents the
weakest factor in the American social fabric and it is in her
treatment that is to be found the real character of American manhood, black and white. The respect of the average
colored man for his women is a mere flicker, due largely
to the little respect he has for his own color, that is, himself,
and in no small measure to the great value so many place on
a white or near white woman, while Southern chivalry not
only refuses her the title of Miss or Mrs., but through her it
would reduce mankind back to the promiscuous level of the
brutes. Southern Chivalry while keeping the cold, watchful
eye of a duenna on the white woman arrogates to itself the
right to flit from Negro woman to Negro woman. What in
the sight of universal justice is the difference between the
polished Southern Chevalier with a white wife and one or
more Negro concubines, and a coarse Negro with a Negro
wife, and one or more concubines?

The age of consent is fixed at 14 in South Carolina for
says the late Senator Tillman "Negro girls would take advantage inevitably of white men and boys who had sexual
intercourse with them." (Letter to the Maryland Suffrage
News).

The treatment of the colored woman by the white men
of America, as a mass, will make sad reading for future
Americans.   R. H.

LETTER XIII.

My Dear Trent:

Concluding remarks to Part I as I promised.

That it is the Caucasian and not the Negro who desires intermarriage is best proved by a consideration of the psychology of anti-marriage laws. Against whom are they designed, Negroes or whites?

The vast majority of whites will tell you that they are to keep the Negro away from the white woman—the epidemic of Jim Crow bills following Jack Johnson's marriage to a white woman is a strong indication. But anti-marriage law can be directed only against the whites for the whites belong to the upper social stratum and as such have the stronger option of refusal. They must approach the Negro and not the Negro them.

But that it is the white woman who desires the Negro rather than the Negro her, is the secret thought of the white men. As early as 1860 when the Negro was still a slave, the Democratic party fearing emancipation had as a slogan, "Should you like your sister to marry a big buck nigger?" Again, the very first question one white man will ask another, when there arises a question of giving the Negro a square deal is still this same question differently worded. This slogan with its up-to-date version shows, by the way, not only what little respect they have for the discriminatory powers of their sisters but it is a revelation of their own feelings. Feeling, only too strongly the attraction of the black woman they fear for the white woman. There has been no talk of "Your son's marrying a black woman," a condition far more likely to occur, illegally.

And these laws and hindrances act as a stimulus. Nothing shows more clearly the inherent selfishness of human nature than its continued interference with innocent love affairs. The father or mother who in their youth would most strenuously object to interference by parents will in their turn dictate whom their son or daughter should marry. Mankind, in its love affairs, knows pretty well what it wants. Love chooses us, not we it.

> "Love gives itself and if not given,
> No genius beauty, state nor wit,
> No gold of earth, no gem of heaven,
> Is rich enough to purchase it."

White men often do all in their power to depreciate black men, telling often the most ridiculous tales, but taking pains, however, to omit that which would furnish the most convincing proof, leaving colored women alone.

In reading some pornographic literature the other day, I came across a story in which a white woman was relating her experiences with a colored man, and she confessed that her attraction had been greatly influenced by the attitude of the white man toward colored women.

In concluding Part One of my theory, I think that all the facts support Sir H. H. Johnston when he says:

"The mass of the race if left free to choose would prefer to mate with women of its own."

The male Negro instinctively respects the white woman and as long as she respects herself is safe. And even sometimes when she does not. Many a Negro, not at all a model of virtue, has a sense of honor in this respect as fine as that of Joseph of Bible times. The sleeping-car porter cannot be too highly commended for this. I speak from intimate knowledge. Irregularities between porters and passengers are as rare as they are frequent with the white train crew. The records of sleeping-car companies will bear out my statement.

The black man desires the white woman not for what she is, but what she represents, while the white man desires the black woman, not for what she represents, but what she is. But for the glamor and novelty arising from prejudice, the American, like the African, Negro, would wish little or no contact with white women.

R. H.

PART TWO—LETTER XIV.

My Dear Trent:

I now come to the second division of my theme: the esthetic value of the skin color of Caucasian and Negro, respectively.

As is well-known, a very large number of white persons have an aversion for a black skin. So, too, has the native African for a white one. Let us consider some of the reasons.

1. The striking difference makes the superficial mind to think that the difference in color must have a corresponding difference in the essential human qualities. The little English boy whose great surprise was to find that a black man took food in the same way as a white one, and the little African girls who would touch Winwood Reade's skin, and run away shrieking, reflect, in their actions, one and the same phase of mind. Maupassant in "Boitelle," tells how the neighbors shied at the sight of a black girl, and the Africans as we saw ran away at seeing a white man. Now it is apparent that the whites and horses who shied at seeing a black man for the first time and the Chinese of the interior and the blacks, who on the other hand, shun a white skin are all in this respect at the same stage of psychic development, have all the same degree of animal fear.

Beliefs and conventions are products of the environment. With the Africans, ghosts and signs of illness are white. With the natives of Coromandel, God is black and the devil white. With the whites, white is a sign of purity. A good black man has a white heart. The white man's heaven is a place of dazzling whiteness. God and the angels are white people dressed in spotless white. The devil of course is black. To get into Heaven one must, of course, be white, a fact which probably accounts for the inky brother singing with full-throated fervency, "Now wash me and I shall be whiter than snow."

2. **A matter of training.** As the brain of the child is
born blind, and gradually acquires insight with age, one
can teach it anything, that Z is A, and Y is B, and so on.
Let the child so taught grow to a certain age say eight and
then meet one who has been taught the alphabet rightly, and
it will stoutly maintain that Z is A. If such a child has
strong will power it will become angry and even wish to
fight, for this knowledge has become a part of the child,
yea, the child himself and to deny it would be to deny his
own self. Give me a child until he is seven, say the Jesuits,
and we care little who has him after. I attribute this to
the fact that the brain attains its chief development at
seven and that impressions up to that age are distributed
over the whole area of the brain, while subsequent ones find
lodgment only in the interstices. If the child is not endowed
with an investigating turn of mind or does not happen into
another environment, the brain, the fibrous tissue holding
the brain cells, as also the cellular matter become so rigid
from lack of exercise, that it hasn't the physical force necessary to match theory against theory and just as the weak
stomach must reject foods, however appetising and beneficial
to others, so the weak muscle-bound brain must reject truths
however stimulating.

Many white persons have a dislike for colored persons
that they cannot be rid of. Like the religious enthusiast of
any faith, Christian, Jewish, Mohammedan, they will say,
"Say what you will but I can feel it right here in my heart."
But had these persons been reared in an opposite environment they would have felt the prevailing views just as deeply. The son of the most devout Mohammedan, if reared
among Christians, will be a Christian and vice versa.

That color is only incidental and that any other notion
would act as strongly is proved by the dislike for the Jew.

A European friend who is very fond of colored people
tells me that the mere sight of a Jew troubles him, that
he would never sit by a Jew in a street car, and would no
sooner think of handling one with his bare hands than he
would a rat. One day on the sleeping car, a rather clean-
cut young fellow travelling with his parents and his sister
upon seeing a fine-looking young Jewess, told me in the

most shocking language, how he would like to despoil her just for spite.

Many light-complexioned Negroes have a strong aversion for black persons, which, in social centers in the West Indies is often stronger than the aversion of the white for the black, as depicted by Victor Hugo in "Bug-Jargal." The near whites of Jamaica are much more prejudiced toward the blacks than are the English people. The would-be's are usually the worst, the most violent.

But the best answer to the theory of instinctive repugnance, is that this repugnance sometimes does not know when to act instinctively and has to be shown, as when Caucasian Gentiles will associate with Jews or light-colored persons quite blithely when they do not know them to be such. As soon as they learn it though, instinctive repugnance begins once more to function.

One of the reasons why many white persons can never overcome their dislike for a black person is that as children their mothers used black men to frighten them. The same holds true of the African. Untutored African mothers, as Dudley Kidd tells us, frighten their babes with white men, and they grow up disliking them. On the other hand, Kidd tells of an instance where a Kafir was very fond of white men because one of his earliest memories was a white man's tossing him on his knees, and permitting him to search for candy in his pocket.

Black and white children, who grow up together, have no color aversion, although they nearly always drift apart in later years, for the same reason that the rich boy will later shun his poor chum. I remember seeing in Provident Hospital, Chicago, a black baby and white one romping together in utter disregard of the doctrine of instinctive repugnance. Southerners, who grow up with Negroes do not dislike a black skin. What they do most heartily detest is the thought that under that black skin there is a possibility of progress. The Southerner has been taught that the Negro is supposed to fill a certain place in life, and to see the Negro out of that place is to violently disrupt the ideas in the Southerner's brains to cause him to deny those thoughts which have now become a part of him, the man himself. Take the colored man away and the Southerner, as is proved by the late exodus, will violently protest, for in addition to needing him as the stomach needs the hand, he needs him as a setting for his egotism—a feeling expressed by the little Southern girl, who naively confessed that were the Negroes taken away, why, she would have no one to be better than.

The following observation of Bacon is peculiarly applicable to the Caucasian, especially of the South:

"Men of noble birth are noted to be envious toward new men when they arise. For the distance is altered and it is like a deceit of the eye that when others come on, they think themselves go back."

Attempts to prove Negro inferiority today, arise from jealousy. The attitude of the white man toward the Negro is very much like that of the teacher's pet toward a new boy who shows signs of intelligence.

Having seen some of the causes for color antipathy we will proceed to consider the esthetic value of color.

Skin-color, as Darwin demonstrates, plays an important part in sexual selection, and most of us whether we know it or not are so bound by considerations of sex that it is the rare soul that rises transcendant to its influence and determines to look on life through the eyes of common sense. A proof of this is to tell any man of a woman, and the first question, if he is not too old, will not be whether she is intelligent or well-disposed, but whether she is good-looking. Most men, even the gallant and chivalrous Southerner, will skip around enthusiastically for a pretty simpleton, but have a hypocritical greeting for the plain, intellectual one. Dis. like for the Negro is in no small measure a matter of sex dependent, as I showed upon early training.

But we will endeavor to place ourselves outside the influence of sex and consider the color of the Caucasian and of the Negro quite apart from this influence. As it is, my valuation will be individual and I can only hope that some of my ideas will harmonize with yours.

Now, in paint colors those generally conceded the most delightful are not the basic colors, red, yellow and blue, or black and white. It is the delicate tints of these colors that afford us esthetic satisfaction. And so I think it is with human colorings, which, I must point out, is not beautiful, that is, if the colorings of fishes like the Rainbow Trout, the

Dania Rerio and the Hemichromus Bimaculatus; of butter-
flies; and even worms with their rich iridescence is. Take the
two extremes, black and white, the one with superbundant
pigment, gloomy, depressing, the color of soot; the other with
every particle of sunlight bleached out of the skin, and
sometimes with lifeless straw-colored hair; and the color
of pork. The Yorubas call a Caucasian a peeled man. The
truth of this observation is evident, when one considers a
black pig before and after scraping. Pork and soot are of
themselves, unesthetic considerations.

And it is equivalent to this lifelessness of color that
blondes appear old much earlier than brunettes, and are
altogether unfit for the tropics, where their skin soon turns
a dirty yellow. There are, however, some blondes who have
a fine and exquisite texture of skin, like to glazed ivory,
which is most pleasing when accompanied by a soft dainty
pinkness, not redness, that blends harmoniously into the
cheeks. When, however, the pores are large and coarse,
especially when unaccompanied by a ruddy glow, blond often
assumes a cadaverous and fretted appearance not unlike
the hue of a cold storage chicken. This is markedly so with
blondes who are unfortunate to be unhealthy. Persons of
fair complexion generally show their emotions and illness
more visibly than others. Similarly, though black is such
a depressing color yet some black skins are rich, handsome,
glossy, a beauty often enhanced by teeth, remarkably white
and even. Such persons are markedly attractive when they
keep themselves neat and clean. Black men, I feel, ought
to pay special attention to cleanliness. The mind associates
blackness with that which is soiled, and thus a well-groomed
appearance not only belies the popular belief, but offers a
pleasing contrast.

Maurice S. Evans, in "Black and White," in South
Africa remarks of the Zulu, "When thoroughly washed and
duly anointed there is a peculiar richness about his color
which makes the somewhat anaemic color of town-bred
European look sickly by comparison."

There is something, I notice, oppressive to the senses in
any group of persons entirely white or entirely black,
especially when dressed in dark-colored garments. One of
the most chilling and depressing sights, I can recall was

when at the Barge office in New York City, I saw two or three hundred Scandinavian immigrants sitting in rows with their white faces ghastly from the long voyage, and all clad in black and with black shirts and black neckties.

There is a great variety of tints among the whites. Look at any twenty and it is rare to find any two alike. The observer will also note the general coarseness of the texture of skin which many women try to hide with the smoothing effect of the powder rag in the bosom or bag. Some cheeks with a rose tint as also some bosoms and shoulders are very attractive provided one does not see too much of them as when evening gowns are worn. I think most white women appearing in evening gowns unesthetic—color too glaring, too obtrusive.

And not from color alone but from the standpoint of physique. Most modern women, quite apart from color, are singularly unfitted in physique, when judged by the Greek standard to expose their arms or shoulders. I think that if the wearers of evening gowns were to feelingly study statues like the Venus de Medici or the Dancing Bacchante, they would endeavor to cultivate lissome arms and firm well-rounded shoulders, such as one rarely sees except among circus girls. When evening gowns are worn one may commonly see anaemic, fatigued skin drawn tightly over scrawny shoulder blades, sometimes dotted with boils or the scars of healed boils. A sight that chills the esthetic beholder. Human coloring, as I pointed out, is not beautiful, and I feel least of all is a white skin so. The shoulders and upper limbs of most women, I think, look at its best, when covered by a very light gauze—a delicate shade of pink for the blonde, and a light creamy tint for the brunette. Black too, is very fetching and the Spanish girls produce an entrancing effect with the mantilla. Consistent with the thought that human coloring when seen in large areas is not beautiful is the fact that the color and the texture of the silk in which ankles are encased plays an equally important part in the attractiveness as does form.

There is, however, a certain wistful beauty in the pallor of some white skins—a delicacy and fragility that reminds one of the hands, especially the fingers of the invalid—the beauty of decay. There is, in general, a certain daintiness and effeminacy about a "white" epedermis, which though not unpleasing in woman is decidedly so in a man, and the manly men seem to sense this as they usually pride themselves on a coat of tan. The heroes of stories are generally bronzed. Paleness in man or plant means lack of vigor. The bleaching out of man or plant means its progress toward decay. Some recruits clad in abbreviated togs playing football made me feel as I noted the whiteness of their skins that it was out of place that such daintiness should be engaged in so rough a game. Some clerks with the usual pasty complexion of those who follow that calling went off to join the army and came back to visit with the tanned ruddy glow of health and the others were loud in praising their appearance. As they clasped hands and I noted the contrast between browned hand and pale anaemic ones the justice of this admiration came home to me. A white man looks doubly nude and is out of harmony with the landscape except in winter, while a brown or brunette fits more harmoniously, except also in winter. Darkness of complexion gives an appearance of greater strength, and regiments of black men even of similar stature, look sturdier than white ones.

A white skin is unfit not only for the tropics but for the summer temperature of northern climes, which often causes it to blister, while a black or brown skin is unaffected.

In the South, the skin of the whites, even of young girls tends to become parched and to crack especially on the wrists and the nape of the neck. On the napes of some Southerners may be seen regular crisis-crosses of dirt accompanied someties by ugly blotches of brown. I wonder whether this is the origin of the term, "cracker."

Among the mixed-bloods there is a heterogeneity of colors, not many shades of which are pleasing, especially in the city-dwellers. The gloss and texture of their skin is too often ruined by the alkali in the numerous brands of bleaching powder, so that one person presents in his or her face quite a large assortment of complexions.

Just as the truth lies between extremes, so I think the most beautiful and restful human coloring lies between the extremes of black and white—brown.

There are, I judge, four points necessary for a beautiful

skin—fineness of epidermis, smallness and regularity of pores, uniformity of color, with or without a ruddy tint in the cheeks, and freshness. In my opinion, the most esthetic shade is a soft smooth light shade of brown when accompained by a ruddy glow which blends evenly into the complexion. I have noticed some colored persons but not many like this. Such are probably a mixture of half Negro and the remainder Caucasian and Indian—a complexion found much more frequently among the Hindus of the north, who, as a rule, are characterized by the fine texture of their skins. Jewesses of southern climes also are noted for their fine complexions, and many of them remind me of Byron's ecstatic poem, "The Girl of Cadiz."

But for general beauty—color, facial contour and weave of hair, I think the most incomparably beautiful of all human types are to be found among the quadroons. In the type, I have in mind the blunt visage of the Negro has rounded out the angular frigidity of the Caucasian aspect and the African color has toned down the over-naked whiteness of the European. As I note the remarkable compelling beauty of some colored women, eclipsing as I think that of white women, because a beautiful colored woman is far less likely to have the glint of haughtiness in her eye, a condition that spoils so many beauties, I am convinced that one great contribution of the Negro to American culture is undoubtedly physical beauty.

But whatever the spiritual influence of color may be on us, the fact remains that if a black skin be associated with badness it is, as Milton so poetically expressed it in, "Il Penseroso," also associated with wisdom, and that if whiteness be associated with purity, it is also associated with frigidity—merciless Nature as expressed in the climate of the far North.

Black is more justly an emblem of purity than white. While white is fleeting, black represents durable purity. One so strong as to absorb or repel other colors, the other, the slightest touch and it is no more.

Black as a color of human beings, is also of superior value whether judged from the standpoint of climate or economy. But just as the silver in an American dollar is worth less than that in a Mexican one, but has greater purchasing power because of the superior wealth of the United States, so while a black skin is really more valuable than a white one, the white has greater value because of the superior wealth of brute force behind it.

Judged from the standpoint of esthetics, color, black or white, belongs on the remotest possible by-path of value. Those who put such a strong, not to say a moral value on color, had they come into the world seeing it a difference of thumbs, instead of color, would, I am convinced, have been just as ardent supporters of the doctrine of inferiority based on thumbs.

That, then, such a little thing as color, should be endowed with such piercing significance, making or marring the lives of certain citizens, and with the consent, active or silent, not only of the masses, but of the classes, the most cultured, this, I say raises grave doubts as to the quality of American intelligence. One fact is evident, its inferiority to that of the French, for instance.

For color prejudice is really crudity—paucity of world variety in the mind. To show its infantile nature. Once in a tropic clime, I saw some children playing. One little girl picked some berries and stained her face and hands a reddish brown. Her three year old brother upon seing her thus changed, ran away, yelling lustily, but as soon as the stain had been washed off he was no more afraid. Now it is evident that since he was not frightened at his sister before she stained her face or after she had washed it, that it was not the intrinsic human quality, but only the color to which he objected, due to a change his infantile intellect could not comprehend. It is evident that the attitude of this child, the untutored African who shuns a white skin and the Caucasian of reputed refinement who shuns a cultured man because of color, are all the same. The untutored African seeing the nearly uncolored skin and not realizing the fundamental unity of the human race is frightened until he sees that it entails no fundamental difference. Stanley says that while he was wondering whether the Uhombo were human, they too were doing the same. Similarly certain whites not grasping the truth of the oneness of the human race imagine that the possessor of the black skin is fundamentally different from them. What is called instinctive repugnance is a second nature due to fear of competition. That it is not instinctive is proved by the fact that were some great calamity to happen to the South, some strong invaders perhaps, see how quickly they would want to make common cause with the black man, just as the so-called instinctive dislike for horse-flesh vanishes in time of famine or the yellow dogs of Eastern Europe that are kicked and buffeted around in times of peace, become in war times a very dear friend, in the pot. In the presence of the German enemy white American soldiers quite forgot a life time of dislike for the black man.   R. H.

PART THREE
LETTER XV.

My Dear Trent:

We now come to Part Three of our theory:
Predominant Negro characters, physical, spiritual, and
intellectual. I shall take them in order.

Jean Finot in his "Race Prejudice," one of the world's
great books—a book as scholarly as it is humane says:

"Very frequently the so-called inferior races show precisely the physiological properties, which, by revising all pre-
conceived methods place them at the head of humanity."

Prognathism, for instance: One of the leading arguments
in support of Negro inferiority is that he has a prognathous
or protruding jaw. But this supposed defect, Prof. Arthur
Keith of the Royal College of Physicians and Surgeons now
values as "healthier dental development," a condition, "which
modern Europeans would willingly share with him, because
of its functional merits." Another is texture of hair. But
as Finot argues, if man in his ascent came through the apes
then the Negro through texture of hair is further away from
the apes than is the white man or any other race, in other
words, if the doctrine of evolution is correct then the Negro
of all races, has the most superior hair. How silly it is,
then, that so many of our men and women should render
themselves prematurely bald, by scorching out the roots of
their hair merely to follow a fashion.

Books to stock a large library have been written detailing the superior qualities of the Caucasian, but so far
as I know very little has been done toward a collation of
the better qualities of the African, physical and spiritual,
although the libraries are full of scattered information. To
be found fault with has been the lot of the black man. If
preaching, admonishing, and physicking with good advice
made men good then all Negroes like so many Enochs and
Elijahs ought to be translated to heaven alive. No people

have ever been so continuously criticised, so dosed with admonition and good advice. Hebrew mythology tells us that Noah dosed the ungodly for a hundred and twenty years, but the Caucasian has been doctoring the Negro nearly three times as long.

This fault finding seems to be the habit of most of those, black and white, who deal with this farce. The thoughts of all but a few gravitate to this pessimistic trend, with the result that after nearly three hundred years, the African's bump of badness has been very carefully dissected and every bad trait even to the remotest capillary been so carefully charted that for once we have a branch of human knowledge that is really complete. All the bad that can be said has been said. In view of this then, I crave your indulgence, while I discuss two physical qualities which place the Negro at the head of humanity, and in the term Negro, must also be included as Sir H. H. Johnston points out, the Negroid. The so-called Negro was gathered from all parts of Africa and Africa has hundreds of races.

These qualities are genesic, or sexual vigor (1), and endurance.

Life, regarded metaphysically, that is, as we feel it, resolves itself into two creative forces: sex and intellect—the first predominantly the sphere of woman, the second, of man.

Now, of these two creative forces sex is infinitely the more important as without it there would be no intellect. Sex is the sole link between us and past and future generations. Intellect, especially in the varied and exquisite manifestations of the Fine Arts, is merely a by-product of sex, even as the oil, saccharin, perfume, and the esthetic and altogether delightful shades of dyes are by-products of the combustion of common coal. Pure or poetic love and estheticism in their tenderest, most delicate manifestations are exhalations of sex. Sex is to animate Nature, man, plant, and beast, what life is to the individual. As the desire to live is paramount in the individual, so the desire to live through sex is the paramount, perhaps the sole purpose of Nature. As the individual desires nourishment, through food from the earth, so animate Nature desires nourishment through sex. Blood is the quintessence of common earth;

the reproductive fluids, the quintessence of blood, and intellect fed from the quintessence of the reproductive fluids.

Sex exercises a vital influence on even the most minute details of life, and its health and vigor is as necessary to love—the harmony of the home, and the peace of the individual—as the sweetening quality to the use of sugar.

"All thoughts, all passions, all delights,
Whatever stirs this mortal frame,
Are but ministers of love,
And feed his sacred flame."

But in spite of the overwhelming importance of sex, genesic vigor, though privately admired, is publicly a thing to be ashamed of—a fact that has been given the cue for many anti-Negro books. But the ancients, Greeks, Romans, Babylonians, Phoenicians and others used to worship sex as testify phallic relics to be found in every part of the habited world. And I might add, that in spite of all repression, we, today, are approaching a perverted sex worship in our cheap, obvious sex plays and stories which in times past, were kept from the masses by dislike for the printed word, but now, impressed on their minds by the motion picture, and in the animalistic style of woman's dress.

We are taking this simple animal impulse which if it is to act at all must do so spontaneously, and are building upon it bastions of psychological mystifications and hindrances.

How then has sex so fallen from grace, and is now mainly the butt of filthy stories and jokes? Mainly through the influence of Christianity. Christianity, especially puritanic Christianity, except in a few rare sects, regards everything we like, as harmful: only that which we do not like is good for us. Christianity then, seeing the great sway of sex on human feeling, used all its influence to render disgraceful the only way possible of perpetuating the race.

Result, this cosmic force which mankind is utterly unable to suppress has been diverted into harmful channels—in hysteria, morbid sensitivity, and in the conditions that obtain in many young ladies' boarding schools, and nunneries with their ingenious devices to simulate nature, thereafter ruining health and dispositions. The greatest disgrace that can ever happen to any woman, perhaps forced by the conditions of civilization, to remain unwedded is to exercise the functions of motherhood for which Nature especially made her and without which her life is a dread and dreary blank.

And it was quite in accord with this policy that Christianity discouraged bathing as it made the body attractive. Baths were as noted for their absence during the Dark, Middle, or Christian Ages, all synonymous, as for their presence under the Pagans.

And, of course, the most devout Christians were those who kept themselves filthiest. Today the man who does not bathe is made to do so; then, he would be praised for his great religious devotion. St. Hilarius never had a bath. St. Agatha smelt like a polecat and praised God for it. "St. Simeon Stylites," says White, "was in this respect unspeakable. The least that can be said is, that he lived in stench and ordure unspeakable." Travelers not infrequently complain of the odor of savages. The Courts of the Middle Ages were as great offenders in this respect. The great epidemics of those times were due to lack of bathing and sanitation.

Intellect, as I said, is an efflorescence of sex. Even as we may extract poisonous gases and explosives from coal or perfumes and candies, so may we have noxious or beneficial effects from sex. We may distil poisons to ruin life or intellectual effort to stimulate and bless it. It is as potent a power as imprisoned steam and will find or make a vent, as we see it, in the religious demoniac, the lasciviousness of Messalina or Brigham Young, or in the irresistible and gigantic intellectuality of Byron, Tólstoi and Dumas. It does appear as if a high degree of the World Will, sexual vigor is necessary to superior accomplishment in philosophy, art, poetry, and those arts which demonstrate the working, not of the intellect, but of Nature. It is the ebullition of this force and no other that makes the irresistible Nietzche to utter triumphantly, "Now rageth my hammer relentlessly."

And in this most important life principle, the Negro is richly endowed, possessing perhaps more than double the vigor of the average Caucasian. Although I have abundant confirmation of this gathered from the most reliable sources, oral and written, yet centuries of convention crystallized into statutes might render it impolitic to state them in this letter. I might say, however, that Havelock Ellis quotes a French army surgeon to show that the white man in Africa is powerless to excite the Negro women.

Theal, says of the Bantu, "A people possessing greater power of increasing their number rapidly than any other on the face of the earth."

Rightly, or wrongly, I interpret the animalistic appealing style of modern woman's dress as a sign of the waning genesic powers of the more advanced Caucasian groups. The tendency of modern woman is to go suggestively clad. Compare the styles of today with those of fifty years ago. The efforts of the fair sex in this respect are like those of the cook, who arranges his dishes to stir the jaded appetite of the bloated gourmand. Every line of woman's dress is designed to allure, to entice. Is it by chance that every detail is so nicely worked out—bust so arranged as to exaggerate or show its fullness, or skirt so fitted as to accentuate the hips and just long enough to show exquisitely stockinged calves, padded or otherwise. Let anyone compare the effect of a dress of this order with that of a nun.

Nor would the citing of my suppressed data be necessary to prove that the Negro possesses a greater degree of genesic vigor than the Caucasian. Sufficient it would be to quote the opinion of anti-Negro authors, who, under the spell of puritanism seem one and all to be convinced that sexuality and vulgarity must necessarily be one and the same.

R. H.

* * *

APPENDIX.

Genesic vigor is thus something to be proud of despite the attitude of Christianity and that puritanical prudery and hypocrisy which has attained its highest development in English speaking countries, where a very large number are never wearied of pointing out the French as a hideous example of immorality. Those who are most addicted to what is considered objectionable not infrequently attempt to detract attention by loudly proclaiming the faults of others. It is characteristic of the hypocrite that he never looks within. Class for class, there is nothing to prove that the Negro is a whit more immoral, sexually, than the whites, despite the number of books in the libraries to the contrary. Sir H. H. Johnston has pointed out that the Negro is as fully capable of chastity as any particular lot of white men and Asiatics. The conclusion of Havelock Ellis and other distinguished psychologists are that the conditions of civilization increases the sex instinct. Nor does that argue a greater vigor. Weininger has pointed that while a certain well-known group is much more occupied with sexual matters than the "Aryan," it is notably less potent sexually— a fact which had previously come to my notice by observing the actions of members of this group on sleeping-cars.

Nor do I intend one word of this letter in extenuation of loose conduct. There is no doubt whatever that the mass of Negroes is by far too much occupied by matters of sex. A very great deal of what the anti-Negro authors say in this respect is only too true. Large numbers of our young men of the better class could, I am convinced, spend their time far more profitably to themselves and their people than at present. But as I have endeavored to show works of art, are blossoms of sex, and I am confident that as the group advances, this vigor, a great deal of which is now spent in debauchery and howling at revival meetings will be diverted into channels that will make its members the leaders in intellectual accomplishment here in the United States. I shall later on discuss the charge of immorality against the Negro.

I would suggest that the virtuous writers of the lack of virtue in the Negro as also those who find such huge consolation in the thought of Negro immorality divert their attention for a while and consider their own people. Dr. Robinson of the Medical Review of Reviews tells of the applause from the members of the South Carolina Medical Association when one Dr. McIntosh spoke of the great immorality of the Negro. White critics of the Negro will, I am sure, render themselves doubly useful in also trying to improve the morals of their own people, since the Negro's fault is to a large extent, but a carbon copy of the white man's.

Whites who animadvert upon the morals of the Negroes, must be, I am convinced, quite uncognizant of that of their own people. Schopenhauer, one of the wisest of the world's wise men, in speaking, as I have reason to believe, chiefly of whites, says, "Half their lives, men are whoremongers and the other half cuckolds, and women must be correspondingly classed as betrayed and betrayers."

Certain ethnologists point to the phallic rites of certain African tribes as bestial but I am sure such have never considered the Domus Vettorium, or the red-light district that existed in Chicago as late as 1914, a light whose diffused beams are still burning brightly in that city.

The Crown Prince of Dahomey, Africa, while on a visit to Chicago, was twitted by a reporter for having six wives. The prince in rebuttal argued that he was at least not worse than the white man. It is true, he said, in effect, that I have six wives, but I am legally married to each, and to them, I confine my attentions. The white man, on the other hand, is legally married to only one, while he has five others to whom he is not married.

And this is a fact. The very commonest thing in Caucasian civilization is adultery. Solomon acquired a thousand wives and I am convinced were many a modern white man to undertake like Solomon to provide for each of his loves the rest of her life, he might very nearly equal the Judean monarch.

Despite the attempt to saddle the origin of syphilis on the Chinese or the Indian, it has yet to be proved that it is not a European product. Anyway today, syphilis occupies as prominent a place in European civilization as literature, firearms and the Bible. A wandering Jew, the white man carries this plague wherever he goes. Syphilis is the real white man's burden—the hall-mark of European civilization. Ricord, the famous syphilologist estimated that 80 per cent of all men between fifteen and sixty had some form of veneral disease; and he was not speaking of black men. At any juvenile court or hospital in any large city may be found large numbers of white girls as young as ten with all forms of disease contracted through venery, and I once saw white soldiers standing in line to get into a house of infamy.

White reformers, who single out the Negroes would find excellent food for thought, were they to read the newspapers. and consider how many cases of adultery, such as that of the Waukegan school teacher and a society doctor; of a university professor and the wife of an army officer are taking place, sub-rosa, minutely.

In conclusion, if the great failing of the Negro is sexual immorality that of the more advanced races of the Caucasian, as I shall later prove, is that which is much worse; self-abuse in its many forms.   R. H.

LETTER XVI.

My Dear Trent:

Corresponding and necessary to the African's genesic vigor is his sturdy physique.

J. H. Balmer, at the convention of the International Lyceum Association as reported by the Chicago Herald, Sept. 16, 1916, says:

"The Zulus are the physical superiors of other races. A male Zulu has the strength, endurance and body of a prize fighter in the pink of condition. Their shoulders are broad, their chests deep, their waists slim. Their women are the strongest females propagated."

Maurice S. Evans, "Black and White in South Africa:"

"Those who are acquainted with the members of the Zulu Royal House, are impressed with the extreme symmetry of form and distinction of feature which belong to many of them.

In physique, physical vigor and power of endurance they undoubtedly rank high, whether as compared with any other primitive people, or with Europeans . . . A really fine Zulu is a magnificent specimen of a man often perfectly built, judged from a European, aye, even from an ancient Greek standard, deep chest, broad shoulders, perfectly shaped limbs, well-shaped hands and feet . . . . Very few are malformed, a fine torso and beautiful rounded limbs belong to nearly all."

Winwood Reade, "Savage Africa:"

"They (the Krumen) are men of the Herculean type, a contrast to most savage races . . . . they are the most athletic race in the world. They are Goliaths of strength and statue."

Rev. R. R. McBriar, "The African at Home:"

"You probably never saw a finer specimen of the human frame except in statuary. Nor is the work of nature disguised for the round limbs and graceful figure of these

Foolah girls have no covering. The narrow strip of cloth tied around their loins only prevents their modesty and yours from being offended whilst you look at their unartificial gracefulness."

Miss Vesalius, "Yankee Girls in Zulu Land:"

"Walking along the street one day, I observed a tall Zulu dressed to his knees in a sleeveless shirt. He stood about six feet high and carried a knob cane. As he approached the very earth seemed to shake under his powerful tread. And as he passed and breathed out, an "umph, umph," at each step a cold chill went all through me, and I felt for the first time that the strongest pale-face was a mere child, compared to this mighty black man. His physical force was so great that as he passed I felt as if my spirit has been overthrown by a wave of power."

And the same holds true of the Negro in the New World. Native soldiers in the West Indies are easily the physical superiors of the English ones. According to the Chicago Evening Post, Nov. 7, 1917, the rejections for physical reasons for the draft at Camp Lewis was between 3 and 4 per cent for Negroes and between 10 and 11 for the whites.

The Negro, with his small hips and broad shoulders, approaches much nearer the perfect male type, than the Caucasian with his feminine pelvis.

For every hundred Negroes called in the draft, thirty-six were accepted for service, as against twenty-five for the whites, due probably to superior physical qualifications

Chicago Daily News reports Dr. W. K. Jaques, draft examiner, as saying:

"Among the hundreds of men looked over by our examining board, the Negroes without a doubt average highest for perfect specimens of the physical human creature. They were the tall strong Jack Johnson types, some of them. They came from people who have worked hard and played in the open air."

In my next, I shall speak of that second quality which places the Negro at the head of humanity, endurance.

R. H.

LETTER XVII.

My Dear Trent:

To speak of the Negro's powers of endurance.

Maurice S. Evans, "Black and White in South Africa":

"The Red Man, the Polynesian, the Maori, unable to stand the breath of the white man and the change in environment he brings wither away, the black man persists. New conditions are introduced, they change him not; new ideas, he wonders and goes on his way; new diseases arrive, he still increases in numbers . . . . One has to but look at the physique of the ricksha puller, the plump comely forms of the strings of native girls walking through the streets, the absence of anaemic or of malformed among them to recognize we are dealing with a race of exceptional physical power and virility."

Joseph Burtt, supplement to the address of the Right Hon. Sir Chas. W. Dilke, Universal Race Congress:

"Unlike the Red man of America, or the Maori of New Zealand, the Negro of Africa appears to be an enduring world race. His physical vitality, ready emotionalism and joy in life show a vital youth as the hopelessness, lack of fecundity and joyless pursuit of materialism point to the declining age of more advanced nations."

Of all living organisms man is the only one that can suffer a radical change of environment and survive. It would follow then that the variety of mankind that thrives best in any given part of the world would be the hardiest. The white man, even under the most favorable living conditions, cannot thrive in many parts of the world. Dan Crawford says: "For the fearful fact must be faced that all things European degenerate in Central Africa. European provisions go the bad, European fruits, European dogs degenerate. So, too, do European men and women."

Palgrave says of British Guiana: "Field labor and outdoor life are things early or late irreconcilable with European vigor, health and even existence."

Sierra Leone is called "The White Man's Grave."

On the other hand, the Negro will thrive in any part of the world from the frozen North to the frozen South if the living conditions be but half favorable. It is not my purpose to depreciate other peoples, but the history of the Negro in the New World does appear to prove him the hardiest of all peoples. I attribute this to the theory that he is nearer the basic stock of the human race.

Throughout the conflict of the ages, the black man has persisted. Silently, grimly, he has hung even in the face of overwhelming odds—and smiles. When the kind-hearted Las Casas saw the Indian flinching under the heavy burdens of the white man, he suggested the Negro, who has not only displaced the Indian, but the whites, as in Jamaica and Hayti. According to Las Casas, the whites and the Indians of San Domingo dwindled from three millions in 1492 to 200 in 1542. When the English took Jamaica from the Spanish in 1655, the Indian had almost disappeared. One must also remember that the voyage from Africa was made under the hardships unparalleled in the history of travel. Stedman says of newly-landed slaves: "Such a resurrection of skin and bones as forcibly reminded one of the last judgment. These objects appeared to be risen from the grave, or escaped from Surgeon's hall, and I confess I can give no better description of them than by comparing them to walking skeletons covered over with a piece of tanned leather."

Another important fact to be borne in mind is that there is good reason to believe that it was not the best of the Africans that were brought to the New World. Such were very likely to have been from the slave class and from those not strong enough to escape in the raid on a village.

In the United States in 1910, Ireland, with immigrants equal to one and one-half per cent of the total population, furnished in proportion more than 15 times as many paupers as the Negro and the Germans, with 2.7 furnished 3.5 as many. It is true that these whites came from a foreign land, but it is also true that the foreign immigrant has wider avenues of advancement. Moreover, all but 33 of the paupers had been in the country twenty-six years or over.

R. H.

LETTER XVIII.

My Dear Trent:

Am I not forgetting the higher death rate of the Negro, as also his great susceptibility to diseases of the lungs? According to the mortality statistics of 1915, the death rate is: Negro, 23 per thousand; white, 13. I notice the sociologist objects.

I say, in reply, the mortality statistics do not offer an accurate basis of computation. The registration area is mainly in the North and cities of the South. It hardly touches the great rural districts of the South, where live about 75 per cent of the Negroes. It will be remembered that the death rate of the city is always higher than in the country.

That the Negro death rate is not due to climate or to constitutional defects, I shall attempt to prove.

A great deal of Negro mortality is preventable, being chiefly diseases of the circulatory or respiratory systems, while mortality from cancer and other incurable diseases are higher among the whites. A most convincing proof that the Negro death rate is due to forced living and ignorance is the fact that the death rate from hernia is invariably higher among Negroes than whites.

Another preventable is infant mortality. Infant mortality is high among Negroes in the registration area. This is undoubtedly due to lack of care both before and after birth. According to the Medical Record, Jan. 5, 1918, the death rate for Negro babies in the Columbus Hill district, New York City, was 314 per 1,000 in 1915. Intensive efforts were made to check it, with the result that it was reduced to 168.50 in a year. The eugenist of the Nietzche school will perhaps inform us that it was a mistake to save the lives of these babies, that they are of bad heredity, and that in another five years or so they will die. But apart from the fact that sickly children often become robust in later life, is not bad living conditions, the continued weakening of each generation, the principal factor in bad heredity? In the manufacturing city of Manchester, N. H., the death rate for babies less than a year old is 193 per thousand. Is it reasonable to suppose that the whites of this town were originally weaker than other towns in New Hampshire, or in Omaha, Neb., where the infant death rate is only 59.2? And let us suppose it were possible to kill off all the weak persons, is it not reasonable to suppose that it is only a matter of time when the weaker of the strong ones would have bad heredity caused by the greed of the stronger ones? In Europe may be found scores of scullions who can trace their descent from royalty.

I would also point out that the high infant death rate of Negroes has nothing to do with the climate. There is probably no way of knowing the rate of infant mortality among the Negroes in the United States, but let us place it at 168.50, the result reached after one year of preventive effort in the Columbus Hill district, it would yet be lower than that of many German cities. According to the report of the Prussian Medicinal Dept. of 1912, the infant death rate was: In Berlin, 178; Danzig, 203; Breslau, 203; Magdeburg, 202; Posen, 212 per thousand, respectively.

Another of the many instances where care has lowered the Negro death rate is Durham County, N. C., where it was lowered from 23 per thousand to 18 in one year.

The consumptive death rate of the Negro is nearly three times that of the whites, but again climate has nothing to do with it, since the Indian death rate from this disease is about three or four times higher than the Negro, and that of the poorer classes of whites as high or higher. As the 1910 Census reports point out, "The mortality from this cause among Negroes and among certain elements of the foreign stock, including not only the foreign-born themselves, but also their American-born children, is markedly high." The Chicago Herald, March 26, 1917, tells of three hundred cases in one white tenement block. According to the American Journal of Public Health, 8.6 per cent of the whites examined in a house-to-house examination of a certain district in Chicago occupied mainly by the middle and lower classes had consumption.

The reason for the higher consumptive death rate of the Negro over the Caucasian, and that of men over women, I take to be harder living conditions. Nearly every one has latent tuberculosis or has had tuberculosis, as may be seen by tuberculous lesions on the lungs of many healthy persons. Sir William Osler estimates that about 80 per cent of persons have had tuberculosis and Nageli at 90 per cent. "Comparatively few," says Osler, "reach the age of fifty without a focus somewhere of tuberculosis."

Now as long as our intake of energy exceeds the expenditure the body is capable of resisting the attack of the germ. Life, as you know, is a matter of resistance—anabolic forces against catabolic forces. The body is a battleground where microbes wage incessant warfare and we are healthy or sick in proportion as the preservers or the destroyers are in the ascendant. Hard living conditions is the best aid to the destroyers. War, for instance. The consumptive and the cardiac death rate of soldiers who come from the strongest portion of the community is very much higher in war times. The hardships of war stimulates the tuberculosis process in individuals previously clinically healthy. As proof of the increased mobility of the tubercule bacillus caused by war, I give the following figures of death from consumption in Vienna from the Vienna Neue Presse. They are for corresponding weeks in various years. In 1909, 295; in 1913, 236; a reduction of 59. In 1915 it jumped to 286 and in 1917, 448.

That the Negro's death rate from consumption is due to hard living conditions is further proved by the great increase of this disease since the abolition of slavery.

Dr. Coleman says in Kleb's "Tuberculosis":

"Tuberculosis was almost unknown to the Negro in his savage state, and even in his condition of slavery in this country, whereas under his changed condition of freedom, broadly speaking, it carries off three to four of this race to one of the Caucasian."

Proof that the Negro death rate has increased since the abolition of slavery is that in nearly every state of the registration area, while the Negro death rate from infancy up to the age of 65 was higher, yet between 70 and 90 it was lower than the whites.

And no wonder the increase. Set free in an environment of the greatest complexity, utterly unequipped with the necessary knowledge and wealth, and instead of being at the mercy of an individual, whose interest it was to take care of him, at that of the public, who could take all without having to give anything.

That the living conditions of the Negro are harder than that of the whites require no proof, but I will give one:

The report of the United States Department of Labor, October, 1917, in its monthly review, tells of an investigation of the living conditions among the poor classes in Washington, D. C. After pointing out that the barest minimum upon which existence for a normal family can be maintained upon a level of common decency cannot be less than $900 or $1,000, and that "such a sum, moreover, is estimated to permit of nothing more than creature necessities," says:

"The Negroes fared worse than the whites. Of 629 Negro families 180, or nearly 29 per cent, were obliged to keep body and soul together on less than $600 a year, and 472, or no less than three-quarters of the total, lived on less than $900."

On the other hand, of 1,481 white families investigated, only 65 had less than $600 a year; 335 had less than $900, and 710, or nearly one-half, had less than $1,200. Using the poorest of both classes as a common basis, we find that poor Negroes were about seven times as frequent as the poor whites.

I spoke a moment past of a house-to-house canvass among the whites of a certain district in Chicago. Of this, Dr. J. D. Robertson, who conducted the investigation, said, "A study of the amount paid for rent and the low wages received would convince many that lack of money was the root of the trouble."

Climate, as I said, has evidently nothing to do with Negro mortality.

Brig. Gen. Malvern Barnum Hill in the Chicago Daily News, Nov. 15, 1917, says:

"I have been with colored outfits in Montana, through the severe winters felt there, with the temperature dropping to 40 below zero, and have found them as cheerful and with as high health rates as in the tropics. Up in Montana nights, when it is bitter cold and blizzards rage as only they can in Montana. I have passed the quarters of the colored troops and found music, singing, dancing and absolute cheerfulness. Down along the border two years ago on the hottest kind of days I have passed their tents and heard the loud guffaws and noisy banter just the same."

Nor has vitality, for Negro longevity far exceeds Caucasian. As I pointed out a moment past, while the Negro death rate from infancy up to the age of 65 was higher than the white, yet between 70 and 90 it was lower, increasing again from 90, for that is an age few survive, and there were more Negroes to die. According to the census of 1910, there were 2,675 Negro centenarians against 764 whites, a ratio of more than 30 to 1.

Now, when we consider, first, that the Negro is an exotic; second, that the Negro of the New World was from the weaker of the Africans of Africa; third, the hardships of the voyage; fourth, the demoralizing effects of slavery; fifth, the increase in mortality following emancipation; sixth, the brutal living conditions of today; seventh, the incomparable greater longevity; eighth, that a high Negro death rate does not necessarily mean a lower grade of vital force, I may safely conclude that the Negro, as a race, is superior to the Caucasian in physical stamina, and that if, on his entry to the New World, he h ad been accorded at least the treatment of the white immigrant, he would today have been a leading factor in American affairs.

* * *

APPENDIX.

The high Negro death-rate does not necessarily argue a greater health of the whites. To quote from the Report on the First Draft, p. 44:

"Thus it appears that out of every hundred colored citizens called 36 were certified for service and 64 were rejected, exempted or discharged; whereas, out of every 100 whites called 25 were certified for service and 75 were rejected, exempted, or discharged."

As the report points out, the greater number of colored accepted might not have been due to superior health, but one thing is pretty sure, it was not due to exemption for marital responsibility, for Negroes marry more and have more children than whites.

A high Negro death rate might even mean that the Negro as a race is healthier than the whites. Few of us but have some physical defect. The hard-living conditions—ignorance, poverty and exploitation—increases this defect, thus mercilessly weeding out all but the fittest Negroes. On the other hand, the better living condition of the whites—superior food, sanitation, greater means of procuring skilled medical advice, etc.—tends to perpetuate the survival of the unfit among them and the transmission of decayed vitality to their offspring. Conditions reversed, it is safe to conclude that the white death rate would take a huge leap, probably far exceeding Negro. With a little more humane treatment Negro mortality would greatly decrease.

Few seem to realize the tremendous significance of the term "Negro vitality." Let me attempt to visualize it. Now as there are about eight and a half times as many whites as Negroes, and let us say three and a half are friendly, a very conservative estimate; then imagine, if you will, one man, with his bare hands, unequipped with wealth or knowledge, struggling with five well-equipped ones, and not only holding his own, but actually forcing a passage through them.

My conclusion is, therefore, that the Negro is superior in physical stamina. Nearer the basic stock of the human race, for there is good reason to believe that the first human beings were Negroes or Negroid, his foundation is grounded in the World Will, Nature herself, that of the white man in a product of the Will, intellect. The Negro superiority is a natural one, that of the whites artificial, and although Art may conquer Nature, yet Art cannot last. The superiority of the more advanced members of the Caucasian group may be likened to a hot-house plant that blooms well indoors, but weakens out of doors. Segregation laws are an unconscious admission of this inferiority. If a Negro pugilist beats a white one, then as soon as the title is regained black and white must fight no more; if a Negro girl outspells a white one, there arises a hue and cry of accusation against those who brought them together, and they must spell no more together.

It is true that the more advanced groups of the whites

have a foothold in every part of the world, but they must be reinforced from time to time or mix with the natives. The native-born stock among the whites, as in South Africa and the West Indies, are usually weaker than the imported.

R. H.

LETTER XIX.

My Dear Trent:

Having discussed the physical, we now come to the spiritual qualities of the Negro.

Before speaking of them, I should like to make this reservation: I do not mean to infer that there are human beings fundamentally different from others. I accept the teachings of Plato, Kant, Emerson, and other cosmic minds that any one man, no matter what his condition, embodies the Idea, Man, in the same manner that the intrinsic quality of gold is always gold, be it found in the ore mixed with silver, iron, quartz or earth, or in a pure state in the monarch's crown. But environment, fittingly termed the architect of heredity, molds character. Long continued sorrow and suffering can soften the nature of a people and render it sympathetic, as that of the Irish, of Ireland, or a constant stuffing of the ego can make it harsh and arrogant, as that of the Prussian. I also firmly believe that there is a certain point of goodness where a very cruel man and a very kind man may meet on an equal footing, and the converse.

The temperament of any group of people, especially primitive ones, may be most correctly inferred from the nature of their music, for as lightning is the most direct manifestation of the vigor of that subtle inner Thing we call Nature, which is one and the same whether it manifests itself in the noiseless fall of dew or in the irresistible onrush of the avalanche, in the meek and inobtrusive action of a Sister of Mercy who relieves suffering, or in the will of an autocrat who sets in motion the machinery for the slaughtering of millions of his fellow-men, even so is Sound the most direct manifestation of the temperament of Nature, whose children we are. The Greeks sensed this when they attributed to Orpheus the power to sway even the rocks by the charm of his music. Even as one may arrive to know his secret inner self, by

watching the impulses to which he yields, so may he know
his temperament by analyzing the nature of the music which
absorbs him. With this assumption, which I think well
grounded, I shall proceed to deduce the temperament of the
African in America from the nature of the music he makes.
Not musician enough to go into all the subtleties of the subject, I speak from a psychic rather than technical viewpoint.
There are, however, three important qualities which are
obvious even to the layman. These are: gentleness, religious
devotion, and buoyancy of soul, with their respective attributes: goodness of heart, loyalty, and sociability:

Gentleness:

African travellers are unanimous on the gentleness of the
African.

Dudley Kidd, "Savage Childhood":

"The children seem to be born good-natured and cheerful.
It is surprising how little they cry, how easily they are
quieted, and how much of life they spend in laughing."

"The Kaffirs are unfailingly polite in their ways, rudeness or breach of their own ideas of politeness being almost
unknown amongst them. Their ideas of what is polite dif-
fer in some ways from our Western conceptions on the point,
yet all who know the natives in their homes admit that they
are a most courteous people. Not a little of their reputation
for lying arises from their excessive desire to avoid rudeness
or discourtesy in speech.

"The smallest children are taught to be polite and this
constitutes their first lesson. Obedience to parents hardly
needs to be taught, for the children notice how every one in
the kraal is instinctively obedient to the old men; the children catch this spirit without knowing it."

Rev. R. R. McBriar, "The African at Home": "The temper of the Negro is naturally mild and hospitable."

Casati, "The Negroes of Central Africa":

"You have admired the politeness of a Frenchman, but
the Negroes of Kano are not far behind him in urbanity of
manners."

Sir Sidney Olivier, "White Capital and Colored Labor":

"In the matter of natural good manners and civil disposition the black people of Jamaica are very far indeed out of
comparison superior to the members of the corresponding

class in England, America or North Germany.

"And generally in this matter of courtesy, which is essential to the relation of equality, I should be prepared to maintain that the African is by temperament and customs of his race not inferior, but superior to the average Teuton."

Ray Stannard Baker, "Following the Color Line," says of the African in the United States:

"I visited many of the poorer Negro homes and I was often received in squalid rooms with a dignity and politeness that would have done credit to a society woman. For the Negro, naturally, is a sort of Frenchman."

The most striking proof of the African's gentle spirit, however, is the fact that during all the time of slavery, whilst he was undergoing some of the most cruel wrongs with which man has ever grieved man, there was not evolved one single song with a vengeful note in it, and in spite of the fact that these wrongs still exist, they merely having assumed a certain refinement of form in a more refined age, they wait ever ready to let the dead past bury its dead.

There are times when certain of the group become very angry, as it is quite natural for any irritated element to become under similar circumstances, but I speak for the majority when I say that they "carry anger as the flint bears fire, which much enforced shows a hasty spark and straight is cold again."

The great majority of colored people are like the better class of any other group of people—anxious to please and to be agreeable.

In my next, I shall discuss religious devotion. R. H.

LETTER XX.

My dear Trent:

With regard to religious devotion. We find this strikingly expressed in the words and music of what are known as the Jubilee songs, or the old spirituals with their yearnings, beauty and tenderest pathos. Colored people are essentially religious. A great deal of the religion of the lower classes is primitive, that is, the worshipers seem to have no distinct idea of the object worshiped. Their devotion is the expression of spiritual exaltation or depression, and takes forms which to the cultured, if non-philosophic mind, appear rather ludicrous, yet they really have a blind faith in Providence to set all things right, and horror is expressed at the atheist. (See Appendix.)

Buoyancy. This we find strikingly expressed in ragtime. A great deal of this kind of music, it is true, is an adulteration of the primitive music, but I think there are few so austere as not feel like yielding to the sprightly strains of the better class of ragtime tunes, when properly played. However much ragtime may be decried by those of sober minds, the fact remains that it has been a world benefactor. It is a ray of cheer that has gladdened the hearts of men the world over, no matter how cold their clime, or their temperament. The Esquimaux are especially fond of it. Two of the world's most touching melodies, "Suwanee River" and "My Old Kentucky Home," are Negro in theme and character. It is being conceded by an increasing number of musical authorities, native and foreign, that the future American music will be based upon Negro themes and idioms.

If anyone were to ask me what I consider the chief difference between Negro and Caucasian temperament, I would unhesitatingly say buoyancy—the difference between sunshine and gloom. In spite of oppression, the Negro is full of the joy of living. Negro men of eighty can usually laugh with the spontaneity of children. I have worked among gangs of white laborers and Negro laborers and the difference in this respect was most noticeable. One would say it was the whites who were oppressed and the Negro free.

Chas. N. Wheeler, writing from France, says:

"It is this continued singing for every task the day through that makes the colored boys the most cheerful of all the American Expeditionary Forces."

Carlyle detested Negroes, but queer contradiction, the Negro, the man who sings while he works, is Carlyle's ideal of a man.

* * *

APPENDIX.

The Negro is by temperament especially fitted for Christianity because he possesses in a great degree the two essentials: mildness of disposition and credulity.

It is only the man who is not of a grasping nature who will accept Christianity. The Negro is already by temperament what the white man with his churches, and colleges, is trying, apparently in vain, to become, for two thousand years of Christianity could not prevent him from disturbing the peace of that world to which he has been preaching the gospel of peace for a long time.

I spoke also of credulity. I believe that the greatest handicap of the Negro today is too much credulity—too much acceptance of a religious faith of which the great majority know about as much as parrots. They repeat things simply because those who preceded them repeated them, all without a single thought as to the liability of human nature to make mistakes. Christianity is a handicap to the majority of Negroes. As I pointed out, it is only the man of a quiet, unselfish nature who will accept it, while the man who needs it, the greedy man, cannot, by his nature, accept it. Christ himself, more than once, pointed out how hard it was for a rich man to become a follower of his. The acceptance of Christianity by the quiet man thus places him even more at the mercy of the greedy man. It is like making the lamb gentler while the wolf is waiting ready to pounce on him. The Negro needs the teachings of Nietzsche, instruction that will make him more assertive, more defiant.

While church-going is good if no more than for the cleanliness it entails, the human fellowship and the music, I feel
that our preachers, regardless of color, ought to keep pace
with knowledge. About ninety per cent of theological education is a perpetuation of those ideas that belong to the
infancy of the human race, and the false, impossible Jewish
history. A sheer waste of time. A decided handicap in the
keen competition of modern life. Now that we have become
men let us put away those childish notions that belong to
the era 6000 B. C. Were anyone to tell us today of having
seen certain events such as happened in the Bible, we would
laugh at him, yet we blindly accept the word of the most
stupendous liar of all times—Jewish History. Let us say, for
instance, that a Negro were to read in Ethiopian history that
a party of Ethiopians once travelled for forty years, without wearing out the single pair of shoes each had. Would he
believe it? Would he believe it were he to see it in contem-
porary Roman, Carthaginian or Grecian history? Yet some
of our most intelligent people believe it of the Jews, simply
because it appears in Jewish history.

Christ was no fossil. He was as modern as if he were
living today or a thousand years to come, and were he alive,
earnest seeker after truth as he was, I am sure that he
would not be numbered among those who doubt the truth of
evolution or at least believed that that most fiendish fiction
of the mind of man, the Jewish Jehovah, took at one time
a handful of nothing and after whirling it around made a
world out of it.

The preacher, Negro or otherwise, would, I am convinced,
be rendering a far better service to his flock, and to the
human race at large, by stressing social hygiene, for instance,
than by frittering away valuable time in teaching that which
is not only often historically incorrect, but so far as modern
use is concerned is as dead and as useless as the paring from
a finger nail.

In so far as the preacher aims to better humanity by
inculcating the spirit of Christ so far has he my hearty support, but when with his superstition we part company.

"Self-love," says Shakespeare, "is not so vile a sin as
self-neglecting," and Negro temperament most certainly
needs to take that advice to heart. The Negro's greatest
need is to learn how to put himself first.   R. H.

LETTER XXI.

My Dear Trent:

"Goodness of heart" is the next of the spiritual traits to be discussed.

African travellers are also unanimous about the Negro's goodness of heart.

Stanley ("Through the Dark Continent"), speaking of the most debased tribe he had met and the expression of sympathy of certain of its members for one of his men who had got hurt, says:

"And all at once there went up from the women a genuine and unaffected cry of pity and their faces expressed so lively a sense of tender sympathy with the wounded man that my heart, keener than my eyes, saw through the disguise of filth, nakedness and ochre, the human heart, beating for another's suffering, and then I recognized and hailed them indeed my own poor degraded sisters."

Du Chaillu: "I shall never forget the kindness of the women to me while I was sick. Poor souls! They are sadly abused by taskmasters, are the merest slaves, have to do all the drudgery and take blows and ill-usage besides, and yet, at the sight of suffering, their hearts soften just as in our own more civilized lands."

Winwood Reade, speaking of hunters who had left only that morning:

"The hunters returned in the afternoon and the others ran to meet them and welcomed them as if they had been gone for years, murmuring to them in a baby language, calling them by their names of love, patting their breasts and laying arm upon arm, shaking their right hands, caressing their faces and embracing them."

Goodness of heart is the most important of all human qualities. We admire the brave man, the skilful man, the wise man, but perhaps we might not love any of them, but every one loves a kind-hearted man, even the unreasoning horse or dog. Goodness of heart offers a firm bridge across the abyss that isolates individual from individual. This noblest of all qualities, may, in human affairs be compared to the function of gravitation in universal affairs, for even as gravitation keeps matter and all the planets in their places, and prevents them from flying together and destroying the universe in one grand cataclysm, so does goodness of heart subdue self-interest and maintains harmony between individuals. I feel that Schopenhauer did not pay too high a tribute to it when he said, "As torches and fireworks become pale and insignificant in the presence of the sun, so intellect, nay, genius and also beauty are outshone and eclipsed by goodness of the heart. Even the most limited understanding and also grotesque ugliness, whenever extraordinary goodness of heart declares itself accompanying them, become, as it were, transfigured, outshone by beauty of a higher kind, for now wisdom must be dumb. For goodness of heart is a transcendant quality; it belongs to an order of things that reaches beyond this world, and is incommensurable with any other perfection."

And in this quality Negro character is especially rich. Everyone knows of the unreasoned devotion of the slaves to the family of their masters during the Civil War. Destitute pedestrians in the South always know where to go in search of food and shelter.

A sympathetic nature means, too, a lively and ever-present imagination—a constant and spontaneous putting of one's self in the place of others. As this most chastened, most beautiful form of imagination continues to be lighted up by education, I predict new world-enlightening eras in the development of the Fine Arts by the Group.

The Negro's chief contribution, not only to American but to world civilization, is that quality which the great Keats placed above all others, Beauty—Beauty, physical and spiritual. 　　　　　　　　　　　　　　　　　　　R. H.

LETTER XXII.

My Dear Trent:

Loyalty is the next of the spiritual traits to be discussed.
Sir H. M. Stanley says:

"For me, too, they are heroes, these poor ignorant children of Africa, for from the first deadly struggle in savage Ituru to the last staggering rush in Embonna they had rallied to my voice like veterans, and in the hour of need they have never failed me."

The Committee of Public Information, Washington, D. C., says:

"The loyalty of the African Negro to the colors is touching. As soon as the morale of the service grips him, as soon as he finds himself a part of the great machine moving forward to free the world, his pride and sense of partnership in the business make immediate response."

The most unflinchingly loyal of all peoples have been the Spartans. The Negro is as unswervingly loyal as was he, and without the Spartan's incentive to be loyal. Whether in the war of 1776 or 1812 when he helped to free a country in which he was still a slave, in 1865 when he helped to fight for his freedom and that of the republic, in 1898 when he helped to free Cuba, in 1913 when he fought in Mexico, or today when he has been fighting in France to help make the world safe for democracy,—even without the certainty that his own country is being made safe for democracy—he has always manifested the same singleness of heart. And this is true not only of America, but of the British Empire, France, Brazil, or in whatever country he has found his home. The Englishman living in the heart of London is not more intensely loyal to his flag than the black Briton wherever found. The Roman patrician did not express greater pride in his Roman citizenship than does the West Indian in his British citizenship, and the Senegambian offers his life, "pour la patrie," with as much ardency and devotion as the native son of France.

Sociability. There are three qualities, accentuating the difference between man and the lower animals, viz: the moral law, laughter, and sociability. Of the first even the most benighted Negroes have the foundation—sympathy; the other two are inherent in him to a marked degree. Sociability is perhaps the most admirable of human qualities. Loneliness tends to increase selfishness, while sociability softens and humanizes.

As we saw the unsophisticated Negro shunned a white skin, but the majority of African travellers agree that he is sociable and eager to learn.

John H. Harris says in "Dawn in Darkest Africa":

"The man who would understand the African must get beneath the surface, otherwise he will never know the real sentiments of the native races. If he would probe the mind and the thought of the African he will find no better way than that of living with him. . . . What a wealth of affection, courtesy, and native love is poured at the feet of the visitor!

"Driven by fierce tornadoes, wet, cold, and utterly miserable, I have sought the simple hut of the forest hunter or the fishing shed on the banks of an African river. How warm the welcome! How quickly the good wife will bring forward native refreshment! Let a drop of rain find its way through the roof of the hut on to the white guest and nothing will stop the impetuous host from dashing outside, in the foulest of weather, to stop the leakage. Readily, too, he gives up his rough bed and will curl in the hollow of a tree or beneath its branches, joyfully enduring any discomfort so long as the white man may be made comfortable.

"It is the same at the other end of the scale. Those who discover that terrible disease—negrophobia—creeping over them, often in spite of their better self, will find an infallible cure by staying for a few days with some leading educated native. Their viewpoint will almost unconsciously change under the genial and enlightened conversation of the dinner table, their hostility will melt away under the influence of the natural courtesy of the warm-hearted host. They will begin to marvel that some things should never have occurred to them before, and unless race prejudice closes the observant mind to all reason, the guest will forget that his host is an 'accursed educated African.'"

Dan Crawford says: "Lady, indeed, you must call her, for if you overhear what she says to her equals it is all besprinkled with polite phrases. 'But, Sir,' or 'No, Madam,' the whole being normal tribe usage, not mere make-believe. You might in fact be reading Boswell's 'Johnson,' the respectful Sirs, so marvellously many."

Dudley Kidd: "It is safe to say that sociability is one of the first qualities to be developed in a black child and grows throughout life."

But very often this sociability is detrimental, as it is usually the coarser and less humane whites who are colonists. These not only do not set good examples but often delight in teaching the Negro the worst side of civilized life.

As August Forel says in "The Sexual Question":

"One thing may be regarded as universal, viz: that the sexual depravity of savage races most often arises from the influence of civilized people, who immigrate among them and systematically introduce immorality and debauchery. It is the white colonists who appropriate the women of savage races and train them in the worst forms of prostitution. It is the white colonists who introduce alcoholic drink, which disregards the most virtuous and loyal habits and ends with ruin."

Archibald R. Colquhoun, "The Africander Land":

"The native who in his own Kraal in a state of ignorance is polite, stately, honest, and well-behaved, will degenerate after a little town experience into an impertinent, careless, bad mannered, and often vicious character."

Mary Gaunt: "For years Christianity has been taught on the West Coast and it is now a well-recognized fact that at the coast dishonesty and vice are to be found, while the man from the interior is at least honest, healthy, free from vice."

John H. Harris, "Dawn in Darkest Africa":

"Today one sees the havoc which King Leopold created when he let loose upon the Congo tribes the scum of Europe. None have escaped the infection; girls of tender years, and even boys not yet in their teens delight in practices of which in older days the chiefs would have kept them in complete ignorance for another five years. Upon the women the results have been by far the most revolting, for in the Congo the majority of women have lost their womanhood and have fallen into a daily condition from which even the beasts of the forests refrain."

Sir H. H. Johnston has pointed out that the white man may write in the Negro's brain pretty nearly what he wishes, and without a doubt the Southern white is directly responsible for all of which he is fuming about in the Negro today.

This desire of the Negro to push ahead takes sometimes ridiculous forms—imitation, not emulation. Men and women with a low grade of self-appreciation endeavor to be white or near white by straightening their hair, taking arsenic pills and altogether ruining their complexions by using bleaching powders. Another excellent use for the hair straightening stuff, by the way, is as a paint or varnish remover. While there may be some allowances made for the women, for women, savage or civilized, are mere corks on the eddies of fashion, and also for the near-whites who do this for business' sake, the obvious Negro who straightens his hair, or plasters his face with bleaching powder until at last he looks like a Mexican poodle with the mange, is a ridiculous creature. The spuriousness of the whole thing is so obvious that it is only his shallow wit and utter lack of self-appreciation that prevents him from seeing the servile imposter he is. Regardless of whatever the whites may do toward beautifying themselves, the fact remains that as a people we spend far too much money on beautifying our bodies, money that is badly needed in beautifying our brains. In one issue of a leading Negro newspaper, out of sixty-three business ads. thirty-eight were beautifiers or hair straighteners. As a people, we need first to take the kinks out of our brains, and when we shall have done this, we will see that Nature placed those so-called kinks in our hair for a most just and excellent reason, exactly the same that she gave the whites flossy hair. A very good many of our men and women need to learn that a regime of clean living, plenty of pure water, within and without, and a good mild soap is the most efficient and only beautifier in the world.

If, however, the test of true culture is the ability to appreciate and assimilate variety—things not to be found in one's own circle, the colored group promises an esthetic development of unusual sweetness and power. It is an assimilator in the fullest sense of the term—a world absorber.

The Negro is at present like the young genius who reads and absorbs everything, good, bad and indifferent—detective stories, love trash, etc.—but that same motley knowledge will enable him to most discriminatingly shun what is bad later on. It is only by knowing well what is bad that we can heartily appreciate good. In the meantime let Patience, Faith, be the watchword.   R. H.

LETTER XXIII.

My dear Trent:

As you will recall, we started out to discuss the physical, spiritual and intellectual qualities of the Negro. Having considered the first two, we now come to the third.

In treating this matter of natural mental capacity, my first care will be to shun a very frequent error—the comparison of Negro and Caucasian mentality as based on attainment, since in order to make any comparison whatever we must have a standard—a specific gravity.

That there is no common ground on which to base a comparison of Negro and Caucasian mentality, I shall attempt to show.

Our first task must be to discover where Africans are to be found living in touch with European civilization in large numbers. They are so to be found only in South Africa, and in parts of the New World.

Now since in order to properly judge of a race or an individual, it is essential to first learn of the nature of his environment, the conditions under which he was born, let us look awhile into Negro environment in the places just mentioned.

Intellectual activity, especially as it manifests itself in the Fine Arts, is undoubtedly conditioned by temperature. One has but to live for a short time in the tropics to recognize this fact. There, where it is always warm, one's greatest desire is to loll. Indeed, it is not necessary to go to the tropics for people of Northern climes feel the same aversion to work of any sort on the hot summer days. The reason for this is, that exertion produces heat and as the body already has sufficient heat from the exterior it emphatically rejects the heat that activity would surely engender. The body in its turn reacts upon the intellect. But the effect of heat upon intellectual effort is already acknowledged in the closing of our schools in the summer months.

The best proof of the effect of climate on intellectual effort is that Europeans have been living in South, East and West Africa for nearly three centuries and yet from among them has not appeared one single genius—one man who has attained world-wide distinction in the Fine Arts. That the Negro, a native, and one who has just begun to receive education of a sort should not then have produced any great man or a civilization that could be compared with Europe's is no reflection on them. Yet there have been some distinguished native Africans as Dr. Agbebi, Sir Samuel Lewis, Henry Prentiss, Sir James Thomas.

Another important fact not to be forgotten is that European civilization is the up-to-date version of an ancient Negro culture. That it is superior is no cause for gratulation, no more than that the civilization of a thousand years hence will be judged superior by those then living. So much for Africa.

With regard to the New World.

The Negroes of the New World may be grouped into two regions—those living in the tropics—Brazil, West Indies and Central America—and those in the United States.

Like South Africa, whites have been living in the first region for a long time—nearly four hundred years, and while they have produced warriors and statesmen of considerable fame, a fame in which men of color like Toussaint, L'Ouverture, Diaz of Brazil, and Antonio Maceo have brilliantly participated, yet neither South and Central America nor the West Indies have produced an Emerson, Whitman, or Ward (Lester F.). The great Alexander Hamilton, who laid the foundation of the financial greatness of the United States, although from the West Indies, did not grow up there. Hamilton, by the way, was of Negro descent.

Our next consideration then must be the United States.

The United States is the only country with all the essentials conducive to intellectual development, that is, climate and good industrial and educational conditions. Industrial and educational development south of the Rio Grande is from poor to very bad as compared with the United States. The advantages to be gained from living under British rule in the West Indies has, I feel, been very much over-rated. Although education, principally in its lower grades, is well diffused, yet, the very bad industrial conditions offer no field for cultivated talents. Large numbers of the best and most enterprising spirits yearly forsake those islands for the United States, Cuba, Panama, and Costa Rica. One fact is indisputable, the West Indian in the United States lives on a very much higher plane than in his native land.

The Negroes in the United States may be divided into two groups, South and North. Let us consider the environment in each group.

Prior to emancipation, the education of Negroes was legally forbidden. After emancipation it was desultory, and it is only within the past twenty-five years or so that it is taking shape and beginning to spread. Allowing it to be twenty-five or even fifty years of free development there would still be no basis for comparison between Negro and Caucasian attainment, for the result of education would but make its first appearance in the children. Yet many psychologists attempt such a comparison. For instance, Prof. Morse of South Carolina in a series of tests found that colored children were the mental inferiors of white ones. Now apart from any racial considerations which are likely to influence a test made in the South, for as Prof. Cattell, late of Columbia, has pointed out that if it were to be shown that a certain number of Negro children were superior to certain white ones, there would be little or no protest, but if it were to be proved that Negro children were the general superior of white ones there would be a strenuous one, and apart from the fact that Prof. Miller of Olivet College, Michigan, after equally painstaking tests, found that from the standpoint of original endowment there is nothing in kind to differentiate Negro from Caucasian—apart from these, I say, there would be no cause for pride should the Caucasian child be superior. He ought to be so, since he is far more likely to have been reared in an environment of greater wealth and complexity—his brain thus merely keeping pace with that complexity. Yet another advantage of the white child's would be the greater help and encouragement it would receive with home studies. Colored children are very much less likely of happening into stimulating environnments than do white ones.

As Buckle says in his "History of Civilization in England":

"The child born in a civilized land is not likely as such to be superior to one born among barbarians, and the difference which ensues between the acts of the two children will be caused, so far as I know, solely by the pressure of external circumstances; by which I mean the surrounding opinions, knowledge, associations; in a word, the entire mental atmosphere in which the two children are respectively nurtured."

Fifty or even a hundred years is but a day in the education and development of a race from primitive conditions. It will be remembered that the Britons lived for four hundred years under the milder rule of Rome and did not produce any remarkable men.

White psychologists, who, at this early day, make comparisons, not to find out how to improve, but merely to test which is superior, Caucasian or Negro mentality, remind me irresistibly of the little boy who plants a grain of corn and digs it up the next day to see why it isn't growing.

Not only is Negro education lacking in duration, but also in quantity and quality. According to the Bureau of Education of the Department of the Interior the average in 15 Southern States and the District of Columbia is $10.32 for the instruction of each white child and $2.89 for a Negro one.

The subject of this letter will be continued in my next.

R. H.

LETTER XXIV.

My Dear Trent:

To resume my discussion of Negro environment in the South.

Although education for the whites in every Southern State is very much superior to Negro, yet the whites appear to be making very little, if any, progress. A Northern visitor to the South is forcibly impressed by the general air of stagnation in the average Southern city, in fact, the inferiority in nearly everything. Thriving Southern cities like Houston, San Antonio ,and Miami owe their progress largely to Northern stimulus. That the Civil War is responsible for a great deal of this becalmed condition is quite true, but I think the far juster reason is first, the inherent laziness of the better class of Southern whites, whose "aristocratic" ancestors, after emancipation, were in the plight of the flea who has lost his dog and can't get another; and second, to the great deal of time and energy spent in cussing or discussing the Negro. Just as during the Middle Ages some of the best and brightest minds wasted their time spinning theological cobwebs so many of the brightest intellects of the South expend their energy in the concoction of jim-crow laws, the writing of treatises on Caucasian superiority and the general attempt to head off Negro progress. Suppose the energy, the acuteness, the fine hair-splitting reasoning, the involved distinctions put into the making of jim-crow laws had been put into the cultivation of the soil, in sanitation or in invention, would the South have been the intellectual doldrum it is today? A writer of 1860 said, "The talent of the South runs to sensuality and politics." True then, it is truer now. White illiteracy in Alabama, South Carolina, Kentucky, Louisiana, New Mexico is higher than that of Negro illiteracy in every Northern State.

A writer in the Chicago Evening Post of about Oct. 25, 1916, says with regard to white illiteracy:

"Let us take, for example, the case of Georgia, the 'Empire' state of the South, which is typical of all the states of that section known as the 'Southern South.' We find that a large per cent of its population, white as well as black, is as illiterate as the 'wild man of Borneo,' and that, according to the University Club of Atlanta, illiteracy—white illiteracy—has increased in the fifty-one counties of that state in the last five years. A record that ought to shame a South Sea island."

Lest my statement regarding the intellectual atmosphere of the South be thought biased, I will quote at length from H. L. Mencken, a Southern by birth, and one of the most forceful, capable, and stimulating writers of the day. Mencken says in the Smart Set magazine, of which he is editor:

"Consider, for example, Virginia—in the old days undoubtedly the premier American state, the mother of Presidents and statesmen, the hatchery of national ideas and ideals, the home of the first American university worthy of the name, the *arbiter elegantiarum* of the western world. Well, observe Virginia today. It is years since a first-rate man has come out of it; it is years since an idea has come out of it. The *ancien regime* went down the red gullet of war; the poor white trash are now in the saddle. Politics in Virginia are cheap, ignorant, parochial, idiotic; there is scarcely a man in office above the rank of a petty job-seeker; the political doctrine that prevails is made up of hand-me-downs from the bumpkinry of the Middle West—Bryanism, prohibition, vice crusading, all that sort of claptrap; the administration of the law is turned over to professors of Puritanism and espionage; a Washington or a Jefferson, dumped there by some act of God, would be denounced as a scoundrel and jailed overnight. Elegance, *esprit*, culture? Virginia has no art, no literature, no philosophy, no mind or aspiration of her own. Her education has sunk to the Baptist seminary level; not a single contribution to human knowledge has come out of her colleges in twenty-five years; she spends less than half upon her common schools, per capita, than any Northern state spends. In brief, an intellectual desert, a paradise of the fourth-rate. There remains, at the top, a ghost of the old urbanity, a bit wistful and infinitely charming. But there is no thought under it, no cultural pressure and vigor, no curiosity and enterprise. The mind of the state, as it is revealed to the nation, is pathetically naif and inconsequential; it no longer reacts with energy and elasticity to great problems; it seems fallen to the bombastic trivialities of the camp-meeting and the Chautauqua. A Lee or a Poe or a Jefferson would be almost as unthinkable in the Virginia of today as a Huxley or a Nietzsche in Nicaragua.

"I chose the Old Dominion, not because I disdain it, but precisely because I esteem it. It is, by long odds, the most civilized of the Southern states, now as always. If one turns to such a commonwealth as Georgia the picture becomes far darker. Here the liberated lower orders of whites have borrowed the worst commercial bumptiousness of the Yankee and superimposed it upon a culture that, at bottom, is little removed from barbarism. Georgia is not only ignorant and stupid; it is vicious. A self-respecting and educated European, going there to live, would not only find intellectual stimulation utterly lacking; he would actually feel a certain insecurity. The Leo Frank affair was no isolated phenomenon, no accident; it fitted into its frame very snugly; it was a natural expression of Georgian ideas of the true, the good and the beautiful. There is a state with more than half the area of Italy and more population than either Denmark or Norway, and yet, in thirty years it has not produced a single first-class book or picture or poem or scientific discovery or political or philosophical idea, or other sound contribution to human advancement. If it had been destroyed by an earthquake in 1875, the world would be exactly where it is today. If the whole of its present population were to be transplanted to Mars tomorrow, the news would be of no more interest to civilization than the news that a distillery had burned down in Kentucky.

"If you want to get some notion of the intellectual and social backwardness of Georgia, turn to the last edition of 'Who's Who in America,' and particularly to page 15, on which the assembled *aluminados* are sorted out according to their places of birth. Georgia, with a population of 2,609,-121, contributes 243; Michigan, with a population of 2,810,-173, contributes 551; Vermont, with a population of 355,956, contributes 363. But we forget that Georgia is half black—

we must chalk off the Moors. Very well, let us match that
half of Georgia which is white against that part of the northern populace which is at least half American. (Georgia herself has very few foreign whites.) The result is almost as
striking. The 1,300,000 whites of Georgia contribute 242
Whoswhoistas; the 1,433,375 inhabitants of Massachusetts
who have 'one or both parents native' offer 2,002. In New
Jersey (perhaps the least civilized Northern state) the 1,213,-
601 American and semi-American whites give 'Who's Who'
501 names—more than twice as many as Georgia. Here,
remember, I always regard birthplace, and not place of residence. Georgia is no new state; it had half a million population in 1825, and more than a million before the Civil War.
Yet it is now left far behind, both relatively and actually,
by such new states as Wisconsin, Iowa and Michigan, none
of which got on its legs until after the war.

"Apply any other test and you will unearth the same
sluggishness. The Southern white is falling behind the pro-
cession; not only is the Northern white forging ahead of him,
but also the Southern *procyon lotor*. I turn to page 68 of
the third revised edition of Ely's 'Outlines of Economics,'
just published, and find this:

" 'In the South during the last census decade the number
of Negro farmers increased more rapidly than the number
of white farmers; the acreage of land operated by white
farmers decreased while that operated by Negro farmers
increased 10 per cent; the value of farm land and buildings
owned by whites increased 117 per cent, but the value of
farm land and buildings owned by Negroes increased 156
per cent; while the number of Negro farm owners increased
17 per cent as contrasted with an increase of 12 per cent in
the white owners of farms.' "

With this as the condition of the ruling class, a class
which, on the whole, does its best to crop all Negro aspira-
tions, it is clear that there is no common ground for a comparison of Negro and Caucasian attainment in the South.

In my next letter, I will treat of conditions in the North.

R. H.

LETTER XXV.

My Dear Trent:

To speak of environment in the North as I promised.

In the North, with its comparatively few Jim Crow schools, and colleges, Negroes may get an education, almost, if not on a par with the whites.

But in the North there is a far keener struggle for existence. I say, without hesitancy, that I think the Southerner of the better class has a kindlier feeling for the Negro than the Northerner, provided, of course, that the Negro will smilingly permit himself to be called "Nigger," and generally willing to stay in his place. Northerners tend to practicality. They are after the money. The voice of the almighty dollar is more imperious North than South. Money transactions are much more likely to take place between Negroes and Northerners, than Negroes and Southerners. Southerners tend to sentiment. They are thus kindlier to one another. Northerners have the harsher and more predatory qualities to be found in a commercial race. Northern whites have very little, if any, love for one another, and where would a people as poor and as different in appearance as the Negro come in? But for their color obsession Southerners are usually kind.

Proof of the Negro's hardship in the North may be deduced from the invariably higher death-rate. In the North, the majority of the Negroes dwell in cities, which, as a rule, are death-traps for the poorer classes, those of the North being especially so. I found for instance that in Kentucky, Maryland and Virginia, and the registration cities of North Carolina—the only comparison available—that the death-rate per 100,000 deaths for old age, was, city districts: Negroes, 61.7; white, 67.6. Rural, Negroes, 163; whites, 82.4.

Housing accommodations for the poorer Negroes are bad. It often happens that when white tenants refuse to live any longer in a building it is rented to Negroes, who are often glad to get any kind of place. Landlords take advantage of ostracism to charge sometimes fifty per cent more for rent. Negroes living in the same locality as whites usually pay one-third more rent and I have known this to be true of the same building. A city welfare exhibit in Chicago showed that while the Negro received the least wages he paid the highest rents. It is true that wages are higher North than South but the living is disproportionately higher.

It will thus be seen that the Negro has, as always, the choice of two great evils. In the South, poverty, lack of education and stimulation, and the determination of the whites to keep him in his place. In the North, where education is much superior and more available, in addition to color prejudice, stern living conditions. The poor Negro youth, who sets out to do anything in the Fine Arts finds himself in many instances like the dogs in Esop's fables, who in trying to get at the hides on the opposite bank of a river, attempted to drink up the river, and fell exhausted before they could reach them.

I enclose an appendix to this letter in order to give in greater detail some of the effects of color prejudice on Negro advancement.

* * *

APPENDIX.

In addition to poverty and the usual handicaps often met by ambitious whites, but more so by ambitious Negroes, are the effects of color prejudice, which acts thus:

First, the effect on morale: the benumbing environment of the young Negro, has a far greater influence on his perspective than is generally thought. The white boy starts out with the inspiration that he can be anything he wishes, that he can be president. The Negro youth who would say that would be laughed at, by both white and black, indeed, there is already a comic song to that effect. Everything that can be done is apparently done to impress upon the Negro a feeling of inferiority and it is well-known the effect that repeated suggestions have on even the grown mind. The Roman Catholics while firmly believing in the capability of God to take care of himself, take no chances. They have the Index Expurgatorius, a list of books Catholics are forbidden to read. It is a human trait to look on the dark side rather than the bright and depressing suggestions usually find a fruitful field. I heard a very successful Negro confess to an audience that this early impression had been a great handicap to him, and that he had never been able to entirely get rid of it.

Sir H. H. Johnston in comparing the Spanish Negro with the Anglo-Saxon and French ones says of the first: "He is prouder, more reserved, more self-respecting, shows better taste in dress, has no servility of manner, is quietly courteous and astonishingly brave." The Negro of the United States shows less manly dignity than any other of the many groups in the New World and it is merely because of this. The Negro professional man in the United States on the whole, is much lacking in dignity, by which I do not mean stiffness—and I attribute this to his apprenticeship of porter, waiter, and doorman along with the condition already named.

Another effect is the general indifference of the Negro to his own cause—of course, if he does not regard himself as important then he will not his cause. To this, I must also add his limited powers of appreciation. The color topic is a topic on the lack of freedom. This lack of freedom chafes the educated Negro and his thoughts are most forcibly diverted there, with the result that many speak, write, or picturize this which is uppermost in their minds. Now if such are to do anything above the ordinary in this line, they must have the encouragement and support of the white to a great extent. But the color topic is largely the recital of the faults of the whites and very few wish to hear it, they infinitely preferring the Negro comedian who fits in with their conception. The percentage of Negroes who have not got above the stage of the Vardaman or Billy Sunday type of preacher and politican is relatively much larger than among the whites. Then, too, the mass of the Negroes look to the whites for approbation and the number who will give that approval is, of course, small.

Many of the best types of Negroes will hardly support propaganda on their behalf, although they know that white men are writing books against them, and that the books get into the hands of professors, students, newspapermen, and generally molding public opinion against them. In many Negro homes, I have found the works of the odious Thomas Dixon, but sought in vain for the works of DuBois, Washington, Brawley, or other Negro writers.

Here is a striking example of this neglect; the case of W. H. Ferris. Ferris, a pure Negro, Master of Arts of Yale and Harvard has written a book, "The African Abroad," detailing the achievements of the race wherever found. It is, in my opinion, one of the two most valuable works on the Negro question—the other being Sir H. H. Johnston's "Negro in the New Yorld." Ferris' book is a liberal education in itself and is probably the most erudite work from a Negro author, yet the support he has received from his own people is hardly worth mentioning, nearly all his aid having come from whites, many of which are of national importance. The next time you go to the Lyceum just ask how many know anything about this book.

The man of great intellect is often unfit for those pursuits of life which brings the average man bread and butter. Great cerebral activity often takes the place of that physical activity needed to bring in food and clothing. Nature in endowing a man with great intellect, sometimes stints him in other respects and if he is to do his best, must have independent means or receive support. The poor scholar from the times of Homer has had a hard time, and the poor Negro scholar has a much harder one.

The whites are by no means guiltless in this respect. Their statement that a dead Indian is a good Indian seems also to apply to great scholars, painters or poets. Galton thought the number of geniuses could be increased. I wonder what they would do for a living if it were possible?

Take, too, the case of Blyden, friend and intellectual equal of Gladstone. Blyden was undoubtedly a greater scholar than the much over-rated King Solomon of Bible times. Yet the Negro preacher, the man with the greatest influence says very little if anything about Blyden while he is never tired of expatiating on the wisdom of Solomon. Toussaint was every whit the equal if not the superior of King David, not only as a warrior, but as a man, for, while David stole another man's wife in the most cruel manner possible, Toussaint protected the wives of his enemies; while David,

the man after God's own heart, made unjust aggressions on
his neighbors, on one occasion bringing two hundred sexual
members of Philistines as a present to Saul, in the same
way that white Belgian officials brought in the sexual members of black men, as a tribute to King Leopold, Toussaint
merely protected his own, and with the greatest forebear-
ance. A great deal of the story of David is now known to be
mere Hebraic braggadocio, while that of Toussaint as Wen-
dell Phillips proves was deduced from the lips of his enemies.
Yet the average Negro preacher is never tired of celebrating
and re-celebrating the victories of King David, while one
hears little about Toussaint.

Yet another effect of color prejudice is inter-racial
jealousy. Even as the majority of women are inclined to
be jealous of other women on account of beauty or dress—
beauty placing nearly all women on the same level, the
queen on the throne will be jealous of a comely attendant, the
social queen will not keep a governess or a maid of more
attractive appearance than herself, or daughters—so Negroes
are inclined to be jealous of other Negroes merely because
they are Negroes. Accepting to a large extent the dictum
of the white man that all colored persons are alike, they,
in spite of their contempt for the poor white—a contempt
too noisy to be real—look with disfavor at the advance of
another Negro even while secretly proud of it, in the same
manner that many women are proud of accomplishments
of their sex, but cannot hear without a pang of jealousy
the praise of another's beauty or chastity.

The Negro who tries to be an individual, especially in the
country places, will soon be reminded he is no better than
his neighbors, and that he is not a white man. Among the
better and even the best class of Negroes this jealousy in
a refined form in no small measure exists. No small part
of the outcry against Booker T. Washington was, I believe,
due to the fact that he was a Negro. A great deal has
been written about the evil propensities of the Negro but
the real and only one has been but little, if any, touched on.
The Negro is a chronic fault-finder of his own people. One
hears this petty fault-finding in high and low life. Let one
of the number do anything and so accustomed are they to
looking at themselves through the white man's eyes that

they will blame it on the whole twelve millions, with the usual remark, "Well, you know how our people are, just give them a chance and they will do so and so." A statement equivalent to the white man's, "He must stay in his place." It is true that as slaves we were taught to carry tales, to be jealous of, and to have little respect for one another, but is not slavery now over?

South of the Rio Grande, the cultured Negro, doctor, or other professional is regarded with respect by the lower classes.

This lack of respect for one another is also in no small measure due to a certain misunderstood democracy which prevails in the United States. Certain citizens will not infrequently go out of their way to remind others that they are as good as they are—a sure sign that they do not believe it; where the housemaid considers herself even a little superior to her mistress; where the office boy considers himself the equal of the bank president, and where if a man does not hobnob with everyone, he is soon reminded he is no better than others—in short, where rudeness is often mistaken for independence.

This spirit in its crude form is ably expressed by a cartoon I saw in "Life." An Irishman and his wife both in the clothes they had brought from the old country are standing on the curb. Seeing a well-dressed Negro passing the man exclaims, "Look at that naygur jude Biddy. Maybe he thinks he is as good as us." This spirit, without a doubt, was acquired in the United States for the European of the lower class is usually respectful, regardless of the color of the person.

Similar is the attitude of many Northern visitors to the South, who, as soon as they note the sharp color divisions at once assume an air of great importance, having learned for the first time in their flabby lives that they were of any consequence.

And while speaking of jealousy, I am reminded to say that the treatment of the Negro in the United States is due to nothing less than jealousy. It is similar to the attitude of man toward woman in the matter of employment. Man has been brought up to believe that there are certain occupations and actions his by right of sex, and to see woman, whom he has been taught to regard as weak and dependent, successfully competing with him is irritating to his pride.

Still another blight to the blossoming of Negro genius is the very serious one of lack of leisure. Great accomplishment in any art requires abundant leisure, and no other race in the United States has so little leisure as the Negro. As a group, he works harder than either the whites on the one hand and the Chinese, Japanese and Indians on the other. According to the census of 1910, for every hundred Negroes over ten years of age, who earned a living there were only 64 whites and 70 Chinese, Japanese and Indians.

For every white woman who worked there were about two colored ones. According to the report of the Juvenile Protective Association of Chicago for 1913, eighty and six-tenths per cent of the colored mothers of Chicago, which is fairly representative of Northern cities, had to work while there was only four-tenths of one per cent of white mothers for the whole United States. It is unnecessary to point out the disastrous effect that this is sure to have upon the physique and mental growth of the child.

It is impossible to do fine mental work with a brain exhausted by physical exertion. Until this condition is corrected, a great of the energy that would go to the brain for the production of works of art will continue to expend itself in drudgery.

We have seen then that there is no basis for estimating the natural mental capacity of the Negro as based on attainment.

And not only that, but the difficulties that must first be overcome renders all the more illustrious the achievements of youths like Alain Leroy Locke, who finished the four-year course at Harvard in three with the highest honors possible, and after a brilliant competitive examination won the Rhodes scholarship all at the age of twenty-one; of Groves, the potato king; Isaiah Montgomery, founder of Mound Bayou, Miss.; of Mary McLeod Bethune, who from the most meagre beginning founded the now flourishing Daytona Institute; of Meta Vaux Warrick, who, after struggling against the sternest conditions, has become one of America's leading sculptors. You may be sure that the energy expended by

George W. Ellis, Benjamin Brawley, Prof. Scarborough, Daniel Williams, George W. Carver, the brothers Grimke, and others who find their names in the list of America's most distinguished citizens would have carried them far beyond the mark had they been white. Weininger speaks of one's arising from desolate negation to glorious affirmation. Where the world over can one find more illustrous examples of this than in the Negro race?

"Whatever America has to show in heroic living," says H. G. Wells, in "The Future of America," "I doubt if she can show anything finer than the quality of the resolve, the steadfast effort hundreds of black and colored men are making today to live blamelessly, honorably, and patiently getting for themselves what scraps of refinement, learning and beauty they may, keeping their hold on a civilization they are grudged and denied. . . . I can't help idealizing this dark submissive figure in the spectacle of America."

The spirit of the Negro has the blind endurance of a stream bubbling through the earth, which makes an outlet every time one is stopped. It is Youth; Youth with a cheerfulness and enthusiasm oppression cannot dim. A Negro regiment, the 369th, was awarded that rarest of rare distinctions—the Croix de Guerre or French war cross to an entire regiment,   R. H.

LETTER XXVI.

My Dear Trent:

We now come to our consideration of the natural mental capacity of the Negro.

Numerous volumes have been written on the mental inferiority of the Negro on the assumption that cranial conformation and brain weight are in themselves the final proof of intellectual capability. This is as obviously ridiculous as the assumption that the bigger man is always the stronger. Quality and not quantity make for activity, physical or mental. While it is true that a big man with firm muscles will excel a smaller one with the same quality, yet even then the small man might exceed him in will power. Attainment, intellectual or otherwise, is more a matter of grit, of determination never to give up, than of brains. Macaulay spoke wisely when he said that genius is an infinite capacity for taking pains.

For my part, I fail to see how being brachy-cephalic, dolichocephalic, chamecephalic, orthocephalic, hysepicephalic, ultradolichocephalic, hypercuryprosepous, hyperleptoprosepus or any other term in scientific jargon can have a scintilla to do with the essential qualities of the man. Finot has given this quackery its death blow when after analysing all the theories he finds:

"All these measurements with their imposing numbers and scientific pretensions, as also the theoretic observations, resolve themselves as we have seen into a nebulous doctrine which affirms many things and proves nothing. The exact instruments which anthropologists and craniometrists use offer a fanistic data. The result of their operations are deposited in thousands of volumes, and yet what is the real meaning? In examining them closely, one can hardly attribute to them even a descriptive value, so much do they contradict and destroy each other."

That the average Negro is inferior in cultural development to the average white is obvious. But that he is not inferior in ability to assimilate and apply knowledge is the opinions of those recognized as being most capable to speak on the subject, an opinion confirmed by the phenomenal rise of the Negro in the United States.

For discussion's sake and that merely I will give a few of these opinions in my next letter.   R. H.

LETTER XXVII.

My Dear Trent:

Opinions on Negro mentality, as I promised.

Charles S. Myers, lecturer in Experimental Psychology in the University of Cambridge: "The mental characters of the majority of the peasant class throughout Europe are essentially the same as those of primitive communities. . . .

"With what surprise do we learn that the children of Murray Island taught at the present day by a Scotchman, are judged by him to be superior in arithmetic ability to those of an average British school, despite the fact that their parents' language contained words for one and two only and expressed three by one-two and four by two-two."

Sir H. H. Johnston:

"There is literally nothing in the way of education that the Negro cannot master and master rapidly."

John H. Harris in "Dawn in Darkest Africa."

"Has the colored barrister failed? If so, where? Certainly not in British examinations where brains and energy provide the only standard. I shall probably be told by the critic that he failed in practice. If this be so, how is it that whenever a Crown case comes along the British Government promptly briefs leading native barristers? Has the doctor failed? Again, where? It is not in the English and Scotch hospitals, for he frequently carries a higher degree than he finds among his European colleagues when he returns to the coast."

Felix DuBois, "Timbuctoo the Mysterious," in speaking of the decayed University of Sankore, says:

"We possess the biographies of several hundred of these learned men, who all are related to one another in a more or less direct line. A cerebral refinement was thus produced among a certain proportion of the negraic population which has had surprising results and which as we shall see later, gives the categorical lie to the theorists who insist upon the inferiority of the black races. . . .

"Timbuctoo was not merely the great intellectual nucleus of the Sudan, that is to say, of the Negroes; she was also one of the great scientific centers of Islam."

With the doctrine of inferiority as a stereoscope many qualities considered admirable in other peoples assume an unfavorable aspect when possessed by colored persons. Many persons of otherwise clear reasoning, in this respect, lose their bearings and become hopelessly lost in the fog of sophistry. Heartiness of expression and well rounded laughter are admired the world over, but when exhibited by Negroes are thought by many to be expressions of a coarse nature. Because Alexander Dumas could write with feverish rapidity and in spite of all interruption, could dictate to two or three secretaries at a time and never had to go over what he once wrote, we find John Bigelow attributing this remarkable gift to his African ancestry, but construing that the African's lack of reflective faculties made it impossible for Dumas to go over coherently what he once wrote, and that Dumas had to write after the manner of a clock which when once wound up worked until it had run down. Dumas wrote rapidly and voluminously, and never had to retouch because he had served a long apprenticeship as an historian and had digested well what he had to say in advance.

Bigelow, it is, however, who seems to have been lacking in reflective powers, for the Negro is pre-eminently a philosopher, and philosophical ability is generally regarded as genius in its noblest manifestation calling as it does for reason and reflection in their highest grades. Joel Chandler Harris became famous through the medium of Negro philosophy, which, he said, had come direct from the lips of the Negroes themselves. It is true that at present a great deal of Negro philosophy is humble, but it is penetrating, and only lacks development. The Negro has a keen, almost uncanny insight into human nature, due, no doubt, to his sympathetic nature. The mind of the African Negro is logical, as Mary Kingsley and others who know him well, say.

With regard to the African's philosophical ability, I shall quote from Dan Crawford, the African missionary, who perhaps, knows the native African more intimately than any other Caucasian writer, having lived in the closest contact with them for twenty-two years, without a break. In his book, "Thinking Black," which is one of the best of the books I have read on Africa, he says, "I amglad I went to school with the Negro in his own town. The mere globe-trotter gets a poor enough chance of getting to know the real African. It is only here stuck up amongst his own hovel huts you at last reach the region of hard facts." He goes on to say:

"This pug-nosed Negro of ours has really a brain of phenomenal range. This you can best believe by wiping off the standard that he is poor in numeration for his unit is 'the terrible ten' . . . . another pin-prick this, I know, in the bubbles of tradition. Terrible ten, indeed, for starting so ominously he soon soars into the blue of arithmetic. Thus leaving hundred (Chitota) and thousands (Chihumbi) far behind he reaches the figure for a million (Mudinda). Then, with this as a jumping-ground, he leaps forward into planetary arithmetic in the word Diita, a million times a million. Here, however, his mind calls a halt for man's empire is lost in the numeration of immensity, nevertheless, he tricks the tongue into coining a word—Diona—the 'all' things, that is to say.

"The panther spring of the black brain now baffled, but not beaten, and far up in the giddy heights he starts to dare classify grades of immensity. For this Diona is (1) the speechless, (2) the voice stifling, (3) the measure-defying, (4) the unthinkable, a daring "grand total" idea this of locking up all expanse in the universe into one word. Asked, however to be concrete and not abstract, he says, with an apologetic flourish of metaphor. The grand total of all immensity may be stated in terms of ashes, i. e., all things viewed as separate units must be conceived as the finest powdered ashes known to man. Certainly, here is a man, who deserves better than the Government dog-bark of autocracy; even as here is the real reason of many a black bark answering white-bark in revolt. Depend upon it, ye Rulers with the Rod, this black man is as strong in brains as in biceps.

"We missionaries are accused of making big bouncing assertions about our African's mental ability, and even many a good friend of the Negro claims to be forgiven if he cannot hear of this without impatience. Living as the black man does at the very bottom of Life's hill, the inference is surely a fair one that the African is mentally incapable of seeing anything in the light of an abstract principle. Hence, that weary and too confident assertion that this African of ours cannot possibly be strong in abstract ideas. The late Dean Farrar may be isolated as a serious type of such friendly academic critics, and what I propose to do is to quote Farrar and then proceed forthwith to hand him over to the tender mercies of the two great African grammarians. That is to say, Dean Farrar, a good negrophile is to be viewed impersonally as a very fair type of the average Oxford Don critic who subjectively decides on a question really not in his sphere. Appleyard and the late Clement Scott will on the Negro side be quoted as representing the two extremes of a long line of Bantu study. Of course, as nothing short of philosophy is our pro-Negro claim, we will be slavishly literal and cling hard to this one test word, The Abstract.

"Philosophy is the Abstract. If therefore the African can be proved to be strong in the abstract then the African, ipso facto, is proved to be a philosopher.

"The vaunted wealth of Bantu turns out to be a mere concealment of their poverty. It is due to that utter deficiency in the abstract."
                    FARRAR.

Bantu is highly systematic and truly philosophical."—APPLEYARD.

"The Bantu language has the fullest expression of the abstract one has met with, broad and delicate in its conception, essentially suaviter in modo, fortiter in re."—CLEMENT SCOTT.

"Here, then, we behold in sharp juxtaposition the oldest story of pro and con cross-swearing in the world: Farrar's loose subjective vagaries confronted with hard, stubborn objective data. What a swing of the pendulum from zero to hundred. Is black white or crooked straight? This is the thing honest men yawn over—arm-chair dogmatism in England breaking a lance with the man on the spot—our venerable friend, Quod Erat Demonstrandum, Esq., smiling down so complacently on plain Mr. Quod Erat Faciendum. The former correct and subjective to his finger tips, the latter with his jacket off, sweating over subjective data filling dozens of note books. For Dr. Clement Scott is surely a good example of being very, oh! very much, Mr. Faciendum. If his above-quoted words seems to be exaggerated and sweeping ("the fullest expression of the abstract one has met with") does he not substantiate them all in his 737 pages of genuine Bantu idiom? Tortuous and tricky and to the tune of hundreds of instances, he, it is, who has followed the marvellous Negro far into the penetralia of "thinking black," emerging from it all in a wonder that is almost dismay. Dr. Scott gasps—for "gasp" is the word that Bantu idiom has the fullest expression of the abstract one has yet met with. And philosophy is the abstract remember, ergo, the African is proved to be both brainy and beefy, in fact, he has brains as well as biceps."

To conclude, that there is no difference in inherent mental capacity is clear. The brain of the black man is to the white what virgin soil is to land that has been much tilled. And it is generally conceded that black soil is the richest. The black man has all the possibilities of the white man plus that primitive vigor which in the whites is rapidly being exhausted.   R. H.

LETTER XXVIII.

My Dear Trent:

In your last letter I especially noted this objection from the sociologist: "Is it not a fact that the mulatto or man of mixed blood is usually more intellectual, more pushing than the full blood? In every part of the world—in the United States, Brazil, the West Indies, South, East, and West Africa, New Zealand or Australia is it not the half-blood whether Negro Maori, or Hindu who is the superior? In many parts of the world these half-blood even form a caste from which the full-bloods are barred. Of 139 in a list of 'Who's Who in Colored America,' there were only 15 full-blooded Negroes."

I reply that this statement is undoubtedly true.

How do I account for it?

I think Sir H. H. Johnson has given the keynote to this question, when he says: "The Negroid is a thousand times more touchy, more acutely self-conscious than either black or white."

That is, he is more sensitive, more susceptible to impressions.

Why is he more sensitive?

Well, the half-blood sees his kinship with the whites, feels that what the white man has ought also to be his, and that he ought to receive the same treatment as a white man, result of this discontent, awakening with its consequent development. On the other hand the Indian, Maori, or the Negro feels to a great extent that he is a creature apart. The full-blood Negro is rather inclined to pride himself on Africa. Two poems on "Ethiopia in Exile," have been written by black men. Another reason, the black man has had a far harder time. In every part of the New World, with the possible exception of the Hayti of today, the black man receives and has received harsher treatment than the mulatto—a treatment in which the mulatto participates.

Every time you look at a black face, you are gazing straight into three hundred years of unalloyed oppression.

Again, in slavery times the mixed bloods had better opportunities of being assigned to the gentler tasks of the household, where they consciously or unconsciously absorbed of whatever culture there was. Another factor is that many white men did not neglect their mulatto offspring. Education of the Negro prior to emancipation was confined almost wholly to mulattoes.

Yet the black man has Toussaint L'Ouverture to his credit. To me, Toussaint is the most remarkable figure in the annals of the New World.

Of three colored class orators at Harvard, two were full-blooded.   R. H.

LETTER XXIX.

My Dear Trent:

Am I not evading his question, I notice the sociologist asks, do I not think that the mulatto inherits his intellectual ability and superior will for development from the Caucasian?

With regard to intellectual inheritance, I do not think so. With regard to superior will, I believe so. I shall treat my respective reasons separately.

Schopenhauer, undoubtedly the greatest of modern philosophers, one who comprehended and demonstrated the kinship of all things, animate and inanimate, perhaps with greater clearness than any other, held that a man received his intellect from his mother and his disposition and corporeality from both parents. In his "World as Will and Idea," chapters on "Heredity" and "Metaphysic of the Love of the Sex," he appears to have proved this.

He says in the former chapter:

"If now, we cast upon this problem the light of our fundamental knowledge that the will is the true being, the kernel, the radical element in man, and the intellect on the other hand, is what is secondary, adventitious, the accident of that substance; before questioning experience, we will assume it as at least probable that the father as sexus potior, and the pro-creative principle, imparts the basis, the radical element of the new life, thus the will and the mother as sexus sequior and merely conceiving principle imparts the second element, the intellect; that thus the man inherits his moral nature, his character, his inclinations, his heart, from the father, and on the other hand, the grade, quality, and tendency of his intelligence from the mother. Now, this assumption actually finds its confirmation in experience, only this cannot be decided by a physical experiment upon the table but results partly from the careful and acute observation of many years ,and partly from history. . . . .

Even the old and popular expression, "mother wit," shows the early recognition of this second truth, which depends upon the experience both with regard to small and great intellectual endowments that they are the possession of those whose mothers proportionately distinguished themselves by their intelligence. That on the other hand the intellectual qualities of the father are not transmitted to the son is proved both by the fathers and the sons of men distinguished by the most eminent faculties, for, as a rule, they are quite ordinary men, without a trace of paternal mental gifts."

Galton, I know, seems to maintain the contrary. He says:

"There is a common opinion that great men have remarkable mothers, no doubt they are largely indebted to maternal influences but the popular belief ascribes an undue and incredible share to them. I account for the belief that great men usually have high moral natures and are affectionate and reverential, inasmuch as mere brain without heart is insufficient to achieve eminence. Such men are naturally disposed to show extreme filial regard and to publish the good qualities of their mothers with exaggerated praise."

But when one remembers the attitude toward women, an attitude noticeable in the Bible, for instance, is not this statement of Ingersoll's nearer the truth?

"No matter how celebrated the sons became, the mothers were forgotten. In old times when a man achieved distinction great pains were taken to find out about the father and grandfather, the idea being that genius is inherited from the father's side. The truth is that all great men have had great mothers."

It is well-known that the fathers of Shakespeare, Beethoven, Napoleon, and Lincoln were insignificant men. Booker T. Washington was certainly a more famous man than his father, whoever he was. And so was Frederick Douglass.

Now when we bear in mind that the majority of mulattoes have had Negro mothers is not the view that the mulatto owes his superior intelligence to his Caucasian father at least a matter of doubt?

With regard to will power:

There is, as you know, a distinct difference between the nature of certain Caucasian groups, as the English, Ger-

man, French, European-American on the one hand, and that
of the Negro and the Asiatic on the other, that is, when
taken not individually but collectively. The white man's
nature runs to the assertion of the will, the desire to dominate, to prey on other peoples. The nature of the European has led him to take away land from the people of all
the other continents. He practically owns the world. The
nature of the Negro and the Oriental runs rather to the denial of the will, to be meek, to be ruled rather than rule.
Markedly so is it with the Chinese. The Asiatic and the
African dreams; the European acts. The white man's nature
runs to that side of human nature appealed to in the teachings of Nietzche; the Negro and the Oriental to the quietis-
tic, pessimitic doctrines of Christ, Buddha, Laotsze and other
Orientals. That is why the Negro feels a greater affinity for
Christ than the Caucasian. The white man is by nature predatory, and the two incompatible elements are greed and the
doctrine of Christ or Buddha.

Now since it is evident that a child must have a share
in the natures of both his parents, I therefore say that the
superior development of the mulatto or other half-breed is
due to the acquisitiveness he is much more likely to inherit
from his Caucasian parent, this greater desire merely mani-
festing itself in any of the many walks of life.

But the black man's will power is only dormant, as testi-
fies his endurance. With opportunity, he soon learns to take
the initiative.

In my next, I will treat of the second question raised
in Letter One: Which is superior? the mulatto, whose father
is white, or is black?　　　　　　　　　　　　　R .H.

LETTER XXX.

My Dear Trent:

To speak of the respective values of the two kinds of mulattoes:

Whatever our view as regards intellectual inheritance, there is no doubt that the child gets his virility chiefly from his father's side. Schopenhauer amply demonstrates this in his chapter on "The Metaphysics of the Love of the Sexes." The male element is the more vigorous and vigor is the most desirable of physical qualities. Women admire men chiefly for strength, that is, height, depth and breadth of chest, capable shoulders, and sturdy calves. On the other hand, men admire women chiefly for size and contour of hips and bust, both of which are connected with the reproductive functions—the former for child bearing, the latter for rearing. The basis of life is physical, not intellectual. Nature's first care is the establishment of the physique, just as our first care is the building of the house, and then its adornment with pictures, etc. This is why we mate chiefly by physical attraction, and very little by intellectual. A man may know intimately a hundred women of most excellent character and surpassing intellectual ability, and do not desire a union with one of them, while a passing glimpse of some other woman he knows nothing about might irresistibly move him. Similarly, a woman may know a hundred distinguished scholars and if they be weazened, lacking in manly qualities, unfit for propagating the species reject them all for a stalwart chauffeur of ordinary intelligence. Nature has given and probably always will give, to most men, just enough intellect to live in order that the next generation might be. Food and the sex instinct, or individual and universal nourishment, are the basic factors of life, the uppermost thoughts in the lives of most men and women.

Now to answer this question of the value of the two kinds of mulattoes. Since, as has been proved that the black man possesses a greater degree of primitive vigor, and as the male element is the more vigorous, and further that of the two forces, physique and intellect, physique is the more important, I think the mulatto whose father is black the superior. To this might also be added the theory that a man gets him intellect from his mother. In that case the union of the black man and the white woman would produce a truly "superior" race. The generally milder temper of the black man wedded to the gentler nature of woman would produce a milder, less predatory race than the Caucasian. Which would be desirable. The meaning and end of life is not so much a matter of intellectual and economic development as it is of moral excellence.

Another reason, by no means to be overlooked. The mulatto whose father is black, has a better chance of getting parental care. The black man is far less likely to be ashamed of his offspring. In his liaisons with white women he is less inclined to imitate the rooster, who is most eager around mating time, but soon skips away leaving the hen to care for her offspring alone.

We have had very little opportunity of knowing the mulatto of the white mothers, yet we have records of some famous ones, as Lemuel Haynes, Banneker, Poushkin and Coleridge Taylor.

With this letter I conclude the discussion of the physical, spiritual and intellectual worth of the Negro.   R. H.

APPENDIX TO PARTS I, II, and III.

Before proceeding to discuss the final division of our theory, let us, by way of a general cleaning up, briefly discuss the arguments of certain scientists, who hold views adverse to those presented in these letters. From a large number, I select these four of the most prominent ones:

Lester F. Ward.
Sir Sidney Olivier.
Prof. Jordan of the University of Virginia.

Charles B. Davenport of the Eugenics Record Office,
Long Island, N. Y.

* * *

Ward says:

"When the man of an inferior race strives to perpetuate
his existence through a woman of a superior race, it is
something more than mere bestial lust that drives him to
the dangerous act. It is the same unheard but imperious
voice of Nature commanding him at the risk of lynch law
to raise his race to a little higher level."

As we saw this is not so. The mass of the black peasantry from which the rapist comes, as also the original African, have no desire for the white woman, but for argument's
sake let it be granted that it is the unconscious purpose of the
Negro rapist to raise his race to a higher level, what, then
is the cause of the rape of the black woman by the white
man? For, as has been pointed out in the Medical Review
of Reviews, while the Negro man has raped the white woman retail, the white man has raped the colored woman whole-
sale?

Consistent with Ward's theory of racial superiority, the
only answer could be this: As the purpose of racial intermixture through the man of the higher developed race, and
the woman of the lower is to raise the human race to a
higher level, therefore, the rape of the black woman by the
white man is to raise the human race to a higher level,
while the rape of the white woman by the black man is
for the purpose of raising the black race to a higher level.

Be it so. Now apart from the fact that rape is common
to all countries, that Negro men attack Negro women and
white men attack white women without any possibility of
raising their respective races to a higher level—the percentage of white men who atack white women is far greater
than of black men who attack white women. What of the
rape of French and Belgian women by the German soldiery?
Is it not safe to assume that German or pro-German writers
like Chamberlain, Gobineau and Treitzchke, who regard the
German race or nation and its relation to the other white
races in the same light that Ward views the so-called inferior
races would by this same method of reasoning tell us that
the attack on French women by Germans was the attempt

of Nature to raise the human race to a higher level, but that
when a Frenchman attacked a German woman, he was trying to raise the French race or nation to a higher level?

And more, as the white man is much more strongly attracted toward the colored woman than the Negro toward
the white woman is it not safe to assume that had he, and
not the Negro been the suppressed one, that his attacks
on colored women would have been far more virulent than
has been that of Negroes on white women?

Rape is clearly the result of defective mentality and not
the attempt of the rapist to raise his race to higher level.

* * *

Sir Sidney Olivier says of the union of the black man
and the white woman, "It is bad natural economy and our
instinct very potently opposes it to breed backward from
her."

Let us investigate this instinct upon whose omniscience
Sir Sidney seems so much to rely.

The European noble will instinctively reject a commoner
perhaps his mental and moral superior. It is said that the
captured German officers who belong to the upper class are
much more kindly disposed to their British captors than
to their brother officers who rose from the ranks and are
confined with them.

A member of the Four Hundred whose grandfather probably made his fortune out of glue or corn cure will instinctively reject one not belonging to it, perhaps his superior.

The Austrian in his native land will instinctively reject
a Jew but will entertain and even marry a Negro.

The white Mohammedan will instinctively reject a Christian but not a Negro Mohammedan.

The Brahmin will instinctively reject a European and
consider his touch pollution.

The light colored girl, who is placed in the same class
as the full-blood Negro by the whites, will instinctively and
just as strongly reject certain Negroes for the same reasons
that would prompt a white girl.

The Mandingo instinctively rejects intermarriage with
the Kru, another African tribe.

The Pole has an instinctive dislike for the Ruthenian
and they will not intermarry. The Czech has an instinc-

tive dislike for the German and intermarriage is rare. The Pole, the Czech, the German, the Ruthenian has an instinctive dislike for the Jew and intermarriage is unpopular. Certain savage Africans instinctively reject white persons, however cultured. The infant being reared among beardless men, will instinctively reject a bearded one. The horse who has never seen an elephant, a street car or an automobile will instinctively reject and shy at them, but will cease to do so as soon as he gets accustomed to them.

It is evident that instinctive dislike is a lack of proper training—crudity, and not good biological reason. So-called instinctive dislike by the white man for the Negro is no different from any other form of "instinctive" dislike. It is merely the principle in unconscious nature to become blindly attached to that which it has become accustomed, in other words, sheer laziness to think or to act. Many slaves objected to being freed, and Elbert Hubbard tells of a deputation of slaves, who waited on Lincoln, and asked him not to sign the Emancipation Proclamation. Social workers not infrequently have trouble in getting white slum-dwellers to move, without cost, to better quarters so accustomed have they become to the old surroundings.

What is instinctive dislike anyway? Not infrequently one meets those he dislikes on sight, but with whom he afterwards becomes very friendly. On the other hand, lovers to whom each other were all the world, after a short marriage will bitterly hate each other. Whites who have been reared, or have cast their lot with colored people are often bitterer toward their own than are the colored.

And when all has been said what of the instinctive liking that so many whites have for Negroes? The instinct of the white man potently opposes the union of black men and white women, not so much from fear of bad natural economy as from sexual jealousy, fear of what they regard the superior fascination of the black. White women are generally willing to marry colored men of wealth and position and the white men know it.

Dislike for white women by colored ones is due to the same cause. Colored women fear what they regard the superior attractiveness of white women. Is it not peculiar that the parties who practise amalgamation the most should be so vindictive about it, which practised by others than themselves?

With all the esteem I have for Sidney Olivier, and the gratitude I owe him for his excellent and deservedly great book, one of the most humane and sensible books it has been my good fortune to read; and with all my great admiration and affection for Lester F. Ward, undoubtedly one of the greatest, if not the greatest thinker America has produced, I must say that the arguments of both on racial intermixture strike me forcibly as being a case of good biological fiddlesticks.

Here for example Sir Sidney says about the union of the black man and the white woman, "There is good biological reason for this distinction. Whatever the potentialities of the African stock as a vehicle for human manifestations, and I myself believe them to be like those of the Russian people, exceedingly important and valuable . . . . the whites are now, in fact, by far the furthest advanced in effectual human development and it would be expedient on this account, that their maternity should be economised to the utmost."

Here he compares the Russian with the Negro, and then goes right on to speak of the white races as if the Russians were not white. If there be good biological reason against the marriage of the black man to the white woman, I take it that the Russian would be unfit to marry a woman of his own race. And mark you, the whitest of the so-called white race, lives in Russia—White Russia.

Moreover, the Negro of the United States on the whole, is further advanced than the Russian. The illiteracy of European Russia is not less than three times greater than that of the American Negro.

This flabby and pointless reasoning of many of the best white scholars, I attribute to this: Whenever they speak of the so-called white race, they think of the highest types only. The whites, looking at them in the sense that these scholars do have had the advantage of nearly seven thousand years of accumulated world wisdom, yet a nation like European Russia has not less than seventy per cent of illiteracy, while the American Negro after sixty years of freedom of a sort has reduced his illiteracy from ninety-five to about twenty-five per cent. Blumenbach for the purpose of classification divided the human race into five races, with the full consciousness that it was a purely arbitrary and superficial one, and many scientists lose sight of this fact altogether. Some more of this child-like reasoning in a great man. Ward says: "Although the enraged citizens who pursue, capture and lynch the offender, do not know any more than their victim they are impelled to do so by the biological law of race preservation."

To what impulse, I ask, would one ascribe similar atrocities practised by the Catholics upon the Protestants during the Spanish Inquisition; by the bastard religion of Henry VIII upon Protestants and Catholics alike; and by the Turks upon the Armenians? The biological law of religious preservation, I suppose. Is it also the biological law of race preservation that makes one strong Caucasian nation take advantage of a weak one or a rich man to exploit a poor one?

Again, if there be a biological law of race preservation why should nature prompt the white man to seek out the black woman? The onesidedness of Ward's argument is increased by his speaking of the unconscious but universal sense of the advantage of crossing strains. Racial values like national ones are artificial, often a matter of which side can invent the greatest death-dealing instrument. The sole difference between the race or nation that exploits another and the man who exploits another, is, that in one case, we have group selfishness and in the other individual selfishness. In a word, the "good biological reason," of the Caucasian scientist is what the man in the street knows as "selfishness, greed."

And at this juncture, a thought as to biological value.

Biological value as laid down by Ward and Olivier is really the question of whether might makes right.

To explain. According to the Caucasian there are two races of men, superior and inferior. Now if it were possible to have a man of this supposed inferior race—a Negro, Chinese or Japanese—and a Caucasian, exactly alike in mental, moral and physical value, and possessing the same amount of wealth, in short, differing only in color, facial contour and weave of hair, which of the two would be really

superior? Now let us suppose that each group insisted
that its own representative was superior, insisted so strongly
that they came to blows and decided to go to war about it.
The standard of biological value would then be fixed by the
winner, and only so long as he could hold it by force. But in
the sight of universal justice, the Golden Rule, which
operates the same in every part of the world which of the
two would be the better man? None. The Platonic Idea
of man, that is, that any one man represents the human
family just as any one horse or any one lion represents the
horse or lion family, and the theory of the survival of the
fittest, when applied to human beings, are incompatible
conceptions. This idea that any one man represents the human race also prevents any scientific accuracy in the study
of races. To compare one Platonic Idea with another they
must both be different. We may have an accurate study
of the horse and its difference to a lion, but there can be no
accurate study of the difference between races, say a Caucasian and a Negro as there is no standard on which to base
a comparison.

How many Negroes look like the hideous creature on
the ethnological charts, a type which Prof. Sergi says is an
abnormity, hardly to be seen anywhere in Africa, and how
many whites like the placid Emersonian on these same
charts?

The Platonic Idea is the only true conception, for while
the Idea, horse, and the Idea, lion, are incapable of inter-
breeding, different races of men do mix, and the mixed offspring is capable of reproducing itself ad infinitum. The
race or nation is but the individual expanded. Race, nation,
family are abstractions.

The truest difference between Man and Man lies in language. Go to a country where your tongue is not spoken,
and note how isolated, how cut off from humanity you are.
Go, then, to another, no matter how different in color or cus·
toms, where it is and you at once feel restored.

Race is unity of belief—religious, national or political.

Ethnology, then, has no scientific basis, that is, if science
is truth, accuracy. Ethnology is mainly a mass of differing
sentiments, opinions and guesses, dependent mainly upon the
temperament of the observer. Two travellers will return

from the same country with different accounts. One man might have liked the people and the place, and spoke well of it, the other did not, and that colored their views. The cold, scientific man, if he exists, exists only in mathematics. One thing is sure, he does not exist in ethnology. Ethnology deals with mankind and we either like persons or do not like them, indifference being a milder form of dislike.

The human race, especially the Caucasian portion of it, always has some foolish proposition. The early ages had super-stition, the worshiping of a wooden God, or some beast; the Golden Age had a plurality of Gods, one for each day of the year; the Middle Ages had theology, these same Gods, whether they were wood, plaster, metal, cat, lion, cow, scarab, snake, or ibis, reduced to one grand God, in whose name they squabbled, fought, and butchered millions; and now, the Twentieth Century has Ethnology, the trying to get rid of this last God and the attempt to make a God of certain race or races such as the Germans failed in doing, and the so-called Anglo-Saxon of the United States are trying, indeed actually doing, for whenever it is a question of God or color, it is God who generally takes second place. Proof: Segre-gated churches.

There is no scientific accuracy in ethnology, and least of all, is there in that branch dealing with the Negro-Caucasian question in the United States. The majority of the books have been written by white men, and color conditions force them to take one side or the other, so when Reuter in his book—"The Mulatto"—hints at his scientific accuracy, it is clear that he is being deceived.

All human affairs lead to the question right or wrong. While among the brutes, biological value would be condi-tioned by the survival of the fittest man has the moral law; hence, man's biological value must be a kind heart and good health.

    *   *   *   *   *   *   *

The other day while reading Popular Science for June, 1913, I came across an article by Prof. Jordan of the Univer-sity of Virginia, in which he says:

"I admit the general inferiority of black-white offspring. The reason for the frequently inferior product of such crosses is that the better element of both races under ordinary conditions of easy mating feel an instinctive repugnance to inter-marriage. Under these usual circumstances a white man who stoops to mating with a colored woman or a colored woman who will accept a white man are already of quite inferior type. One would not expect a superior offspring from such parents if it concerned horses or dogs."

Stated thus—that the better element of blacks and whites have an instinctive repugnance to intermarriage, therefore black-white offspring must be inferior—this argument seems indisputable.

But let us analyze it, bearing in mind that the purport of the article is to prove that the alleged inferiority of black-white offspring is not due to the mere fact of mixing.

1. Black-white offspring is not to any great extent the fruit of marriage; nor a present-day product. Humanity's great progress in the art of abortion sees to that.

2. Prof, Jordan's estimate of the better element in black and white seems to be those who have an instinctive repugnance to intermarriage, but this does not necessarily mean an instinctive repugnance to the unmarried relation.

3. Of whom would black-white offspring be inferior, black or white? It cannot be of the blacks because the black-white offspring furnishes the majority of the leading spirits of the group.

4. Since this is so, then the black must come under the inferior type of which the professor speaks, in which case intermarriage would be harmful, which the professor says is not.

5. Weak powers of discrimination with regard to inter-marriage does not necessarily mean weak physique and feeble health, thus while a Negro and a Caucasian might be con-sidered to show weak discrimination in marrying, yet it does not necessarily mean that they are physically unfit, and that their children will be feeble.

6. If aversion to intermarriage is the test of "the bet-ter element," then the Negroes of Africa are superior to those of America for the Africans shun, while the American is generally willing to marry, the whites.

What form does this general inferiority of black-white offspring take, physical, spiritual or intellectual? General inferiority! A very convenient term for any one who talks vaguely on the subject.

I would also point out that Fishberg in his book "The Jew" shows that an argument similar to Prof. Jordan's has been advanced to account for the alleged inferiority of Christian-Jewish offspring—a certain Maretski holding that "persons who are as careless about their religion as to marry out of the pale of their faith cannot expect to have decent children."

And where does the mating of horses or dogs come in? may we ask Prof. Jordan. What relevancy is there between horses who mate from blind instinct or through human agency as when as a mare is again taken out when the foal is but a few days old and persons who do not observe racial distinctions in marrying? If there is any difference between black-white offspring born out of wedlock before slavery and that born in wedlock since emancipation I have never been able to distinguish it, although I know many of both sets.

All I have said is independent of the fact that the statement, "The white man who stoops is of inferior type" is a boomerang. It is the hereditary colonels and majors of the South whose doctrine he is obviously preaching that he is hitting hardest. The mulatto is to a considerable extent the sons and grandsons of the "aristocracy" of the South.

I say he is preaching the doctrine of the colonels because it will be noted he says, "The white man who stoops to mating with a colored woman" but "a colored woman who will accept."

Statements like these are to be unsparingly dealt with, especially when dressed in this clever sophistic garb. The color question is not an academic one, as so many whites seem to think. It has a direct bearing on the lives of men and women. One is dealing directly with human feeling; he is handling dynamite. Let any one say anything about your personality or that of your race and see whether you can receive it coldly. There is no such thing as a cold scientific attitude in the race question. It is a moral issue.

False statements often determine legislators with regard to the enactment of laws, and foreign scholars thinking the source reliable perpetuate these errors by quoting them.

* * * * * * *

Charles B. Davenport, Eugenics Record Office, Cold Spring Harbor, Long Island, suggests as regards intermarriage (Eugenics Record Office Bulletin No. 9): "No person having one-half or more Negro blood shall be permitted to take a white person as spouse. Any person having less than one-eighth part of Negro blood shall not be given a license to marry a white person without a certificate from the State Eugenics Board."

Mr. Davenport at once assumes that all whites are physically fit and all of Negro descent are liable to be unfit. He indulges in the generalization quite regardless of the fact that he says in the same article, "If the demand for cheap labor in the North shall long continue to lure the weaklings of Europe to our Northern cities the North will soon have on its hands as large a problem as the South has now. The problem of the socially fit must be treated not as one of color, but as a problem of the spread of feeble-mindedness and physical weakness in organized society."

Now as every one knows it is not a question of "If the demand for cheap labor shall continue to lure the weaklings of Europe." The truth is the demand for cheap labor has for a long time been luring the weaklings of Europe to the Northern cities. As I have proved the Negro is the superior of certain of the emigrants who came in large numbers to America. Now, if there should be a physical examination for any Negro who wishes to marry a white, ought not there also be one for the immigrant who wishes to marry a native white?

Again Mr. Davenport, after naming certain physical and spiritual qualities which the Negro possesses in a greater degree than the whites, and after saying, "The surest and quickest way for the white man to get them is by mixing with the black," goes on to say, "But it may well be urged what a frightful load of non-social traits would be cast upon society by the presence of such hybrids. Let us enumerate some of these undesirable traits. A strong sex-instinct without corresponding self-control; a lack of appreciation of property distinction (a capacity for which an African origin would hardly have contributed); a certain lack of genuineness, a tendency to pass off cleverness for the real thing, due to inability or unwillingness to master fundamentals; a premature cessation of intellectual development. In respect to health, a relative lack of resistance to tuberculosis and pneumonia, and a liability to form keloid and uterine tumors."

One thing may be regarded sure. Mr. Davenport has picked out the worst of the Negroes' undesirable traits, so we needn't trouble about the rest of that "frightful load." We'll merely examine what he has given, when we will see whether Mr. Davenport's fright proceeds from knowledge or lack of it.

1. "A strong sex-instinct without corresponding self-control."

The Medical Review of Reviews, July, 1916, in speaking of the report of the Baltimore Vice Commission, says: "It tells a tale of lust and sexual deceit and whoredom among the most reputable Baltimoreans, it lifts the cover from a never-ceasing cauldron of sensuality and seduction. Baltimore is a city taken in adultery. . . . The twelve hundred pages of this report are a transcript of the white man's sexual life anywhere; a record which should prevent him from criticising other races."

Then there is the report of the Chicago Vice Commission, a depressing picture of human misery resulting from the tyranny of sex. And remember this is not a tenth. Here we have only those unfortunates whose poverty left them free to the public gaze. It does not touch the lives of those that the vice crusader dares not investigate; nor of the vice crusaders themselves.

Now if the white man with his weak sex-instinct and his thousand of years of culture and exhortation to inhibition exercises such weak, indeed, no self-control at all, is it any wonder that the Negro with his strong instinct does not?

But the truth is no other race exercises less self-control than the Caucasian, for even while proclaiming his superiority to the heavens he readily prostrates himself with any other race with which he comes in contact. They on their part entertain very little desire for him. (See also last part of letter XVII.)

2. "A lack of appreciation of property distinctions."

No one I admit appreciates more strongly than the white man the property distinctions of others; indeed, he appreciates them so strongly that he never ceases to yearn until those distinctions no longer exist, a reason why the jails are full of white thieves. The Caucasian appreciates the property of others so strongly that he has taken away America from the Indians, South Africa from the Negroes, India from the Hindus, etc. Two thousand years ago the white man was told to choose between Christ, the honest, and Barabbas, the thief. He chose the thief, and apparently has not yet reversed his decision.

The number of dishonest whites are, moreover, far in excess of Negro, for the proportion of whites in business is much larger than that of Negro. Theft, in itself, is theft whether the victim is manhandled, or "doped" in the smiling, fawning way of the lower class Jewish merchant.

The great difference between the Negro and the Caucasian in the matter of theft lies in the size of the object stolen. When the white steals thousands mourn; the Negro, an individual.

The Negro is not yet sufficiently educated to be as great a thief as the white man.

3. "A certain lack of genuineness, a tendency to pass off clever veneer for the real thing due to inability or unwillingness to master fundamentals."

This is only too true. But is not the picture drawn by Eduard Von Hartmann of the culture of the whites very much like what Davenport says of the Negro? Hartmann says in his "Philosophy of the Unconscious":

"But now the troop of dilettanti. How little sense and love for the subject, how terrible the want of all understanding, how dependent on fashion—and pretentious show—and yet this dilettante crowding of the arts and sciences! The riddle may thus be read: not for their own sake are the arts sought but as showy tinsel to adorn one's own dear self. The equally unintelligent critics are enraptured at the dress if the person pleases them, and despise it if they have no other ground for flattering the person; they then condemn the dilettante performance the more profoundly the more genuine value it possesses, because they think themselves bound to abash with fitting scorn the audacious assumption that any object may possess intrinsic merit. Of course, under such circumstances the aim becomes to produce startling effects in as many directions as possible in order to dazzle every block head in the easiest way.

"This is the principle of modern education, especially of girls; a couple of drawing-room pieces on the piano, a few songs, a little foliage, drawing and flower-painting, to chatter in a few modern languages and to read the literary scribble of the day, then they are finished. What else is this than systematic instruction in vanity, in every acceptation of the term? And with this juggling can one believe in delight in art? In aversion for art rather which reveals itself from the moment of marriage when vanity no longer gets the bette of love of ease.

"With the boys it is not much better. They, too, must play the part of dilettanti for the sake of their parents' vanity. And then in music as universal instrument, the unlucky encyclopedic, soulless piano. . . ."

This picture, true of European culture, is still more so of the United States with its hurry, superficiality, and bluff. The university graduate, black or white, is too often insipid and hidebound, such personality as he possesses fast bound behind a bristling barrier of cut and dried rules and crammed with information his mechanical brain is powerless to digest. Numbers of white boys and girls after graduation from high school know just as much of the subjects taught as a man who goes through a town on a fast train is likely to know about it. After three or four years' study of French, for instance, the only thing the majority can say fluently is: "Parlez-vous francais."

However, Mr. Davenport's charge against us is only too true, or how else could the majority of colored preachers continue to murder the midnight air with their hoarse bellow uttering "such stuff as mad men tongue and brain not" and not only escape Bedlam but get good coin for it; or how could our large flock of Negro orators, spouters of empty, hackneyed phrases at so much a gush, continue to draw such large audiences? The truth is that too many Negroes are attracted to words rather by their sound and their length than by their meaning—long Latin words and plenty of 'tions. The patron saint of such is undoubtedly Dr. Samuel Johnson with his centipedal words and phrases.

A like superficiality is true of the Southern white, as Albert Bushnell Hart has pointed out in his book, "The Southern South." The best proof of this is the noise-makers that are usually elected to legislatures. The chief qualification often necessary for a legislator of the Southern South is the faculty of being able to volubly string together words and phrases, regardless of meaning, and then direct them against the Negro. Vardaman and Roddenberry, for instance.

4. "A premature cessation of intellectual development."

Every possible effort is made by nation, state, and individual to keep the Negro doing manual work. The Negro youth after graduation from college has a most circumscribed field.

What, cut a lad's already meagre diet, and then blame him for not growing strong!

5. "A relative lack of resistance to tuberculosis and pneumonia."

This has already been dealt with in letter XX and shown to be caused solely by the killing greed of the Caucasian.

6. "A liability to form keloid and uterine tumors."

With regard to the uterine I will quote from "Dudley's Principles and Practice of Gynecology." Chap. XXVI, page 366, as follows:

"The common impression that they are more common in the Negro than in the white race appears to be disproved by the investigations of Howard Kelly and Daniel Williams."

With regard to keloid tumors, if I am to trust my own observation I should say that Mr. Davenport is right. The Negro eats too much pork, has a less variety of food than the whites and living conditions less sanitary.

But are not keloid tumors which disfigure more than harm overbalanced by certain physical qualities in which the Negro is superior? As Mr. Davenport says in the same article, "In resistance to certain diseases blacks are superior to the whites. Thus there is a higher degree of immunity from yellow fever, and though the blacks suffer and die from malaria the death rate from the disease at the Panama Canal has been only one-third to one-fifth that of the whites. Skin cancers, psoriasis and various other skin diseases are rare, to very rare with full blooded Negroes. Dental caries is rare in pure Negroes but frequent in mulattoes. Other special resistances are revealed by the census reports of Maryland. In this state deaths from scarlet fever are relatively fifteen times as common among whites as blacks; erysipelas seven times; diabetes four times; cirrhosis of liver three and eight tenths; diphtheria three times; embolism and thrombosis, also cyanosis, each, three times; nervous disorders and also malformations at birth, each about twice and suicide seven times."

Now does not a greater liability to yellow fever, malaria, cancer, psoriasis and other skin diseases, bad teeth, scarlet fever, erysipelas, diabetes, cirrhosis of liver, diphtheria, embolism, thrombosis, cyanosis, nervous disorders, malformation at birth and suicide not to mention greater difficulty at child birth, or mental defectives, at least balance keloid tumors?

As to the suggested law I shall say nothing, I leave it to the judgment of those who know anything about the situation, or the conditions under which amalgamation is taking place.

Arguments like Mr. Davenport's serve but to accentuate the kinship of revealed religion and the race question as viewed from the Caucasian angle. One might call them twins. Both start from assumptions you must not question, assumptions you must blindly believe. One question and the whole fabric comes tumbling about your ears. Just as the theologian, Christian or Mohammedan, but especially the former, builds edifices of thought, vast, labyrinthine, bewildering on the attributes and nature of God, a subject on which he really knows nothing and on which simple minded and uneducated persons seem to be the best informed, but will tell you with cocksureness how if you will only follow his particular system of religious beliefs what will be the definite result, just so do many biologists build up a perfect system of the grading of life on the hypothesis of sexual selection in order to prove Caucasian superiority. Some biologists tell us, for instance, that the original protoplasm from which man grew, floated naked in the salt water and gradually developed organs of defense. If the protoplasm were the original and only living thing in the world against what did it by sexual selection develop weapons? If the creature that was the progenitor of man had to take to the tree tops to escape stronger animals, how did he live while acquiring the means for climbing? Life, it appears, is a pre-determined set of growths which began in nebulous matter, and has reached so far as we of today are concerned, its culmination in man. Of this series of growths the intellect of man is merely an observer. We cannot fathom the beginning of life, mainly because the intellect is finite and cannot comprehend infinity. To comprehend life in the mechanical way of the scientist we would have to go back to nebulous matter, which in turn leads us back to infinity, which has no beginning. We cannot comprehend life even as confined to our planet for the same reason that a man has no memory of his conception, birth and babyhood. But even as the child will in after years learn something of its babyhood from the lips of others so mankind has been able to deduce something of his earliest life from mud, rocks, plants, the lower animals and the study of archaeology and philology. But the knowledge thus produced is fragmentary and to the highest degree imperfect. For instance the point where the animate blends into the inanimate has never been satisfactorily determined—the connecting link between non-living matter and the protozoa. Again, there is a gap between the invertebrate and the vertebrate that has never been bridged, another between the lower and higher apes, still another between monkey and man; Pithecanthropus is now known to be a gibbon; and yet another between intellect and body, greater even that difference between the animate and inanimate. Our knowledge of life may be compared to one's reading a story with more than half the beginning missing and many leaves here and there in the volume and trying to deduce the rest of the story from what is left, some saying it reads this way and others that. Yet with the absence of this absolutely essential knowledge, with this defective fragmentary information certain biologists with a great deal of cocksureness lay down laws for the instruction of nature, with her billion of years of experience in breeding.

It is surely such Shakespeare had in mind when he wrote:

"Man, proud man

Drest in a brief authority
Most ignorant of what he is most assured
(His glassy essence) like an angry ape
Plays such fantastic tricks before high heaven
As make the angels weep."

Placed among the infinite, the illimitable complexity of life and other natural phenomena the biologist is merely an observer and a purblind one.   There is no certainty whatever that the greater part of knowledge is not incorrect, and that at any time new discoveries might not result that will set humanity facing in the opposite direction as did the discoveries of Copernicus, Kant, and Darwin.   In the opinion of so eminent a biologist as Darbishire, "the satisfaction of the biologist with our current scientific interpretation of life is the satisfaction of the fool with the paradise which he has built."

In spite of the great progress in scientific knowledge no one really knows the determining essence of good biological value especially where the mixing of races is concerned. Mankind refuses to mate like the brutes, a refusal which increases the further he recedes from the brutes.   Here the breeder is confronted with the almost unknown quality of Mind and the desire of the individual for that happiness to be found only in a particular affinity.

While experience in breeding undoubtedly improves dumb animals and plants, the method will not work in human beings, for as Shakespeare has pointed out, "The brain may devise laws for the blood, but a hot temper leaps o'er a cold decree."   In the matter of heredity what can be predicted as to the period of persistence and degree of distribution of either spiritual, physical or intellectual qualities of parents in their offspring?   True abundant data is available but no sure inferences can be drawn from their variegated forms and sources.   Numerous volumes exist to prove that heredity is superior to environment and as many the other way about. Many tell us that the children of thieves invariably develop the habit of stealing at some time in their lives while many assure us that if separated when babes, dishonesty will not develop.

And still less is the biologist or breeder of animals qualified to pass judgment on the Negro and to say where it is good that he should mix and where bad. Prof. Boas, one of the leading anthropologists and probably the foremost one in America says: "As a matter of fact, we know less about the heredity characteristics of the Negro than we do of the other races," and I might add precious little is known of theirs.

Von Luschan, the celebrated anthropologist, says: "As yet we know little about the interesting and complicated psychology of the colored races."

The Medical Review of Reviews points out, "In spite of the long continued presence of an ever increasing colored population we know little or nothing of the anatomy, physiology or pathology of the Negro." Consequently when eugenists and others give such definite judgments about subjects of which so little is known and on questions which are not academic but have a direct bearing on the weal or woe of a group of human beings, they most certainly do not deserve a hearing.

J. A. R.

THE FUNCTION AND PURPOSE OF SEX.

"Nature her custom holds,
Let shame say what it will."
                    "Shakespeare."

"Up, then, follow the truth, not according
to pre-conceived notions, but as nature leads."
                    "Schopenhauer."

LETTER XXXI

The function of sex is first variation, second, reproduction. To produce variety is pre-eminently the first function of sex. Even the casual observer of the aspect of nature cannot but be struck by the infinite multiplicity of form and color. No two races alike, no two nations, no twins, no two sides of one's face, no two voices, no two handwritings, no two trees, no two blades of grass. Variety is undoubtedly the first characteristic of Nature, a strict necessity of her continuance.

To better understand the workings of sexual selection let us consider man, where it is best observable. Think of the great scrupulosity with which the man regards the woman, and she in turn regards him. If reproduction and not variation was Nature's chief aim would this have been so? Would not a man mate with any woman? But everyone has a quite special choice. The unconscious determination of the child to be produced influences this choice—of course I speak of normal love. The case of the soldiers' standing in line to get into the house of prostitution was a perversion of Nature arising out of civilization. Prostitution is one of the products of civilization.

An open example of sexual selection in man is related by Herodotus. He tells us that every Babylonian woman had to go to the temple of Mylitta once in her life and there consort with a stranger. She followed the first man who threw a silver coin in her cup, and could refuse no one. When once in the temple she could not go home until she paid her vows. Some had to remain four years or more, while those with beauty and symmetry were soon set free.

Man is the only land animal that has withstood the march of time. All the other animals have disappeared and have been replaced by new forms. I account for man's perpetuation thus: His superior intellect enabled him to exist in every part of the world, thus enabling his organism to acquire that variety of climate peculiar to every clime. Consider food, the quintessence of earth, for instance. How large a part it plays in life may be realized when we consider that the difference between the energy of the new-born child and that of the grown man is almost solely the result of the food he has eaten.

Climate affects us even in the minutest detail, as in the sound of the vocal organs, the Easterner, Westerner and Southerner of the United States having distinct accents. Here, again, by the way, we see that environment is universal, heredity, a distinctively local question. What we call race is merely the Idea, man, as modified by climate.

The variety acquired by living in different parts of the world, has, I think, been the principal factor in man's perpetuation. Anyway, one fact is evident, the assimilation of great variety food, knowledge, or whatever it be, is necessary for a high grade of human development, individual or racial, moral or economic. The higher the ascent of nature, the greater the complexity. Many of the lowest forms of life are asexual, that is, sexless, a segment of the creature detaches itself and grows, but the higher organisms need the variety that could be imparted only by sexual reproduction.

The higher the organism the more careful the sexual selection. Variety is progress itself. The most advanced people are those with the greatest diversity of blood as the Japanese, English and the people of the United States. Every race, however humble, has its distinctive offering to world culture, even as every man has his distinctive part in the drama of life.

The most stagnant people are those without a diversity of blood, as the Ainos of Japan. A local example is the impoverished appearance of a large number of Southern whites, who, to begin with, were largely of bad stock: young girls with washboard chests instead of the flowing bosoms of young womanhood, razor backed men in which the vertebrae appear as prominently as the beads on an abacus; stork—like necks with huge Adam's apples; arms without biceps and triceps and straight legs without any calves.

Another but less glaring example is the Jew. Fishberg,

writing in the American Hebrew, says that the Jews of Europe have from two to five times more physical and mental defectives than the Christians. According to the Medical Record, Feb. 16, 1918, of seven thousand cases examined at the Clearing House for Mental Defectives, New York City, according to race, the Jew alone furnished a third, having nearly seven times the percentage of the Slavs, who, of all the whites furnished the least. The Slavs in turn had more than double the percentage of the Negro.

Yet another example is the generally diseased condition of many of the royal houses of Europe, who, according to the dictates of politics must marry among themselves.

Mixing of human varieties is as necessary for a continuance of the race as variety of food for the individual especially when we consider that the former is universal, and the latter individual, nourishment.

And this need of variety manifests itself in the life of the individual. The most delectable sweet that ever the mind could imagine, bliss, paradise itself would become distasteful if continually had. Humanity has evolved through pain and nature craves pain, as well as pleasure. We have, as you know, pain nerves and pleasure nerves and both crave nourishment. Nature inflicts pain on us and very often we ourselves indulge the pain nerves by attending tragedies. At a performance of Quo Vadis, I noticed some women weeping and although they were suffering probably their last thought was of leaving.

Another example of the necessity for variety is the case of the very rich with a poor grade of intellect. These are the most discontented of all. Having had almost every thing that wealth can command, and barred by their limited intelligence from ascending to that limitless diversity to be found only in mental development, they not infrequently commit suicide from satiation. Many rich women have the temperament of sitting hens who ruffle up their feathers and set up a shrill squawk at the approach of any one. Solomon who sounded all the pleasures found life was vanity and vexation of spirit. Man is not happy, and there is nothing that can make him so. He will interrupt his moments of serenest happiness to build himself castles of doubt, fear, and suspicion.

With this understanding of the great part that variety plays not only in individual but universal affairs and also bearing in mind what was said of the Negro's superior physical and sexual powers, I will go on to point out why the Caucasian desires to mingle his blood with that of the Negro.

R. H.

LETTER XXXII.

My Dear Trent:

Now for the reasons why Negro and Caucasian are mixing: The Caucasian, as is now generally acknowledged, was dark or brown in color and has gradually bleached out from living in countries with weak sunlight. This is conclusively proved by the fact that the skin darkens when exposed to the sunlight. Detachment of West Indian soldiers stationed in Africa, many of whom are a shade or so removed from black return quite blackened. A season's exposure at the bathing beach will make a white or colorless man into a brown or colored one. On the other hand West Indian soldiers who stay in England usually return much lighter in complexion, and the white man loses his coat of tan in the winter. Shakespeare speaks of the color of the Prince of Morocco as "The shadowed livery of the burnished sun"—a view upheld by modern science. The effect of sunlight on plants is another proof. Chlorophyll, or the green coloring in plants is analagous to pigment in man. Plants that grow in cellars are pale, and as you may have noted invariably stretch toward the sunlight. Placed in the sun they become green again even as the white man again begins to acquire his original color when exposed to sunlight. Pigment or lack of it is undoubtedly conditioned by sunlight.

That the Caucasian was also different in facial contour as, too, was the Negro though to a less extent is well proved by consideration of the new born child. As you know from the moment of conception to the time of birth the child ascends through all the "spires of form." At stages of its development the foetus is like a worm, a serpent, a dog respectively. At a certain stage it actually has a tail. The new born babe is primitive man. Color apart none but an expert can tell whether the new born is Negro, Caucasian or Mongolian. (See Appendix.) Now since the Negro baby is not born black but brown, and a child acquires its facial characteristic later in life,—full lips, spiral hair, and black eyes as in certain Negro races or straight noses and blue eyes in certain Caucasian ones, it is safe to assume that the first human beings were a shade of brown, perhaps reddish brown, and that they had flat or flattish noses, dark eyes and frizzled hair. Whichever way we look at it, from the Mosaic version of the creation of man or the Darwinian theory of evolution, we must come to the conclusion that climate has been the principal factor in the production of the different varieties of the human race, or at any rate give an account for the difference. We cannot argue a special creation or evolution for each, for the difference between the individuals in any given race, and the difference between that given race and any other race is merely one of degree, largely of shape of head. Any way it is now generally conceded that the Caucasian, so-called, is a product of a primitive race.

Now, when we consider that the impulse, and therefore the necessity of Nature is to return to the primitive, to renew herself.—Man becomes dust again, then nutriment for the tree; the tree produces food; food, blood; blood, the reproductive germ. Here man starts again going through all the stages of evolution while in the womb, then the babe or primitive man, then the racial feature, a difference of lips, hair or eyes. When we understand this, I say, I think we have the key to why it was that the German gentlemen of whom Shufeldt spoke said that he preferred a black woman to any white woman he had ever met. It was merely unsophisticated Nature urging him through the color lure to re-establish the brown or primitive color of man. When a Caucasian blisters himself in the sun to acquire a coat of tan and of which he seems proud he is doing superficially what nature is attempting to do by sexual selection. As Schopenhauer has pointed out the "white color of the skin is not natural to man,." and that "In sexual love nature strives to return to dark hair and brown eyes but the white color of the skin has become a second nature."

But there is a deeper and more irresistible cause, the one I had in mind at the beginning of my letter.

This I shall treat in my next.   R. H.

APPENDIX.

This fact gives the lie direct to a story I read in a prominent periodical where a white mother refused to look at her baby because it was born coal black, had kinky hair, flat nose and thick lips. No babies are born black; a reddish brown is the darkest shade, and all babies have flat noses, thin lips, and hair, straight or downy if any.

The Carnegie Institute had two expert pedigree tracers for a year to look up such cases and could find no proof. Dr. Woods Hutchinson has demonstrated the impossibility of an apparently white couple producing a black child. He says: "No individual, either knowing or suspecting that he has some slight trace of Negro blood, need have any fear of having a child born to him darker in color or more Negro in feature than he is himself if he mates with a white partner." If it were possible such instances ought to be frequent because the number of whites who have mates of Negro descent is very large. Large numbers are constantly crossing over to the whites, and the number of persons who pass for or believe themselves to be white must be very large.

Sir J. E. Alexander tells of the white wife of a Dutch farmer in South Africa who became the mother of a Negroid child giving as excuse her being frightened by a black man. But her unmarried sister also became the mother of a similar child, and upon an investigation it was found that the sister had a Negro lover. The most logical explanation of a white or apparently white couple producing a black child is wifely infidelity and if the horror of the woman in the story had proceeded from remorse it would have been far nearer the truth.

A white woman and a black man might be the parents of a black child, but a brown skinned man and a white woman will never produce a black child, no more than a mixture of brown paint and white will produce black. Mere common sense will tell that a child can never be darker than its darkest parent. The plea of a difference in color, however, offers no excuse for the mother just mentioned. For a mother to reject her child on account of color is most unnatural. Birds will hatch and rear the offspring of birds of a different kind, hens will hatch ducks, and carefully guard them, dogs will suckle kittens, black men and women will tenderly rear their children though born with Caucasian features. This story is a terrible commentary upon the cruelty and hard heartedness of certain races of the Caucasian group, especially those of the United States. I say this with the fullest justice, for this attitude, this turning away of a mother from her child on account of its color is not fiction. It is only too typical of the turning away of the race at large from the mulatto, its child.

In my letter on the esthetics of color I pointed out that while white was considered an emblem of purity, it was also typical of frigidity, cold, merciless Nature.

Sunlight or lack of it in the body may after all have a moral significance. R. H.

LETTER XXXIII

My dear Trent:

Have you ever pondered why it is that civilized peoples in spite of their better knowledge for the preservation of life have never been able any more than savages to perpetuate themselves? Why is it that every civilization, racial or national, that the world has ever known, has gone down or out—Ethiopia, Thebes, Egypt, Carthage, Zymbabwe, Timbuctoo, Songhci, in Africa; Scythia, Phoenicia, India, Medo-Persia, Assyria, Babylon, Judea in Asia; Mycenae, Macedonia, Greece, Sparta, Rome, Byzantium, Spain, Portugal, Netherlands, Turkey, in Europe; with Great Britain and France, probably the next to go; Mexico, Peru, Guatemala in America. Add to these a host of minor ones, such as Etruria, Anglo-Saxon, Normandy, Khotan, Vizayangar, Cliff Dwellers, Yucatan, and that probably larger number that lie unexplored or buried in Africa and Asia. Wherein lies the principle for this inevitable decay? For the smaller civilizations, war, pestilence and absorption is the apparent, but superficial answer. But what of those strong enough to absorb these? What of Rome once mistress of the world? What of the United States, which prior to the war of 1914 was the most decadent from a point of natality—the United States so aptly called "the graveyard of the white race."

The key is to be found in one and only one principle, Sex, for that is the sole link between pre-historic man and us of today.

Let us seek therein for the answer to our question.

Whosoever reflects, however little, on life cannot but be struck by the conflict that reigns throughout Nature, aye, even in his own breast, where he is first conscious of it. Life is precious, nerves are delicate and most susceptible to pain, yet all through animate Nature we find forms of life like the lion, tiger, wolf, so constructed that they can exist only by eating others, as the deer, the giraffe, the rabbit. In the ocean the bigger fish eat the smaller ones, who are just as fond of life as they. That this conflict is solar and not planetary, did not arise from the exigencies of our earth, is evident because in the beginning human life, for instance, was not so abundant, as now, and death among mankind could not have been necessary because the earth was being over-peopled. Any way we find this conflict all through animate Nature, the herb preys on crude matter; the carnivora on the herbivora, and man preys on all. But man is also subject to the natural law. Hence as there is nothing higher than man, man preys on himself. It has been said that one man is another man's devil. Truer is it that every man is his own devil. Man wars with himself, and with other men to preserve the eternal balance.

The most deadly form of that conflict that reigns within the human family lies not, as is imagined, in war, but in the conflict between the two creative forces—sex and intellect.

I will treat certain of the more important phases of this conflict.

First of all, man, the most intellectual of the animals treats the females of his species worse than any other. Man has a distinct antagonism for woman and but for his sexual needs woman would soon be crowded out of existence. The martyrdom of woman in all ages, all climes, and among all races conclusively proves this. This, however, is but a mild phase of the conflict.

Far worse is the havoc that intellectual development plays with the organism.

As we saw sex is to animate nature what food is to the individual. We also saw that intellect, the lesser creative force feeds upon sex, that sex is the reservoir from which the intellect drew its forces. Great and prolonged intellectual efforts weaken the sexual powers.

Intellectual effort being creative satisfies nature. The sexual powers of Sir Isaac Newton, St. Thomas Aquinas, and Immanuel Kant, for instance, were completely swallowed up by their great intellect. But all intellectual creations are merely imitatory. They please nature as flattery or imitation pleases the individual. It is like eating the food out of a cupboard, and then replenishing the supply with pictures or carvings of same.

This, it is true, is the conflict as viewed from the ideal. I shall now proceed to show how it applies not only to men of great intellect but to those in every day life.

As intellect develops self-consciousness increases. Self-consciousness makes the individual to stand out from the great mass of nature or humanity, and now arises the desire to sacrifice function, the manner in which nature is nourished for feeling, pleasure to the individual, in other words, the prevention of conception. But added to this desire to sacrifice function for feeling, is that which is much worse: Intellect, the lesser creative force, has a tendency to focus its powers on sex, the greater, and to stimulate it by means of stories, plays, pictures, music, drugs, styles of dress—in short the conditions of civilization sharpen the sex instinct. Along with this stimulation is as I just pointed out, the desire to live as an individual with the result that lust rather than procreation now becomes the motive of the sexual act.

Lust, it must be understood, lies not so much in frequency as in the desire to cheat Nature. The desire to procreate and the desire to produce works of art are one and the same principle. The young genius restrained from producing the children of his brain chafes and frets in the same manner as the motherly woman restrained from bringing forth those of the womb. The desire to indulge in either of these forms of procreation would therefore mean that energy is directing itself toward different channels, that is, the brain and the genitals, and that the volume of desire in both cases would depend upon the amount of energy secreted by the individual. Even as the real glutton is not so much the one who eats his fill, however enormous it be, as it is he who disgorges in order to eat again—as is said the Romans used to do—so lust lies not in volume of intercourse as in the desire to prevent conception.

The difference between the lust of the prostitute and that of the society lady who will not breed is merely the difference between that which is public and that which is private, between a private opium den and one for public use. In this respect your cultured New Englander is more lustful than your packing-house Polock or plantation Negro.

The beasts with but a flicker of intellect, are, with the exception of monkeys in captivity not lustful, and live solely for the nourishment of nature. Savages are much more lustful, and civilized man with his ingenious methods of preventing conception the most lustful of all. Havelock Ellis, Sir A. B. Ellis and others tell us that among certain African tribes the men restrain themselves from conception to the weaning of the infant, a period sometimes lasting three years. Intellectual development tends then to cheat nature of her food. It increases selfishness. Civilized man, especially of the large social centers, does not wish children, finding them a bother and an expense. Women shun the trouble of parturition, child-rearing, etc., and the consequent loss of figure. That a very large number of women have even one child is but the merest of accidents. Ignorant persons are the most prolific. Educated ones the least. College bred women are noted for fewness of offspring.

Nor is this disinclination toward breeding confined to women. The intellectual man has a tendency to shun the maternal type of woman and rather seek the fast woman, the prostitute type—the woman with the wine glass and the cigarette—the type who does not wish to become a mother. Says Iwan Bloch, "The attraction toward prostitutes is one of the most remarkable phenomena in the psyche of modern civilized man, it is the curse of the evolution of civilization." I would point out that this is true not only of modern man but of the ancients. The cultured Greeks and Hindus preferred the society of the hetaira or cultured prostitutes to that of their wives. In a word, intellect shows the apparent purposelessness of Nature, and that reacting upon the will unconsciously destroys the desire of the individual to live on in the next generation. The tendency of civilized man at all times is to look after his own pleasures and let Nature go hang herself.

Lust, the preventing of conception, is to Nature what alcohol is to the stomach of the individual. Both are not only powerless to sustain life, but are injurious. Sex perversion and by sex perversion must be understood every attempt to cheat nature, to prevent conception, pleases the nerves of the individual but adds nothing to the nutriment of the great nerves of nature.

Sexual perversion, the starvation of nature, has been the downfall of every civilization in world ascendency.

Another, a minor, but not to be overlooked phase of this conflict, since its action is more direct, is the tendency to flock to the cities, and leave the soil from which comes all our food. In ten years (1900-1910) the urban population in the United States increased three times in proportion to the rural. Eighty per cent of the people of New England live in towns.

Other phases of the conflict between sex and intellect is the tendency of women to leave the home for the factory and office and the pessimism of highly salaried and intellectual women toward the married relation.

Civilization—intellectual development—means, then, not only a drawing off from the great reservoir of nature but an antagonism toward returning anything to the reservoir. Consequently if such a civilization is to continue it must be reinforced not only by a people with a primitive or near primitive degree of sexual vigor, but also with a weak degree of intellectual fore-thought, akin to that of the lower animals.

To briefly summarize:

Beginning with crude matter, forms of life, in their ascending scale, prey on other forms. Higher forms of nature eat the lower forms, therefore, intellect, the highest form of Nature, preys upon and consumes the body of man, the next highest form.

Civilization, or intellectual development, then is digestion. It is to animate Nature at large what digestion is to the individual. Just as the individual puts food into his stomach so does that omnipotent Force we call Nature places man into its stomach and digests him.

Just as the food in the stomach of the individual changes, the essence going to the nourishment of the body, the rest being expelled, so it is with the digestion of Nature.

The essence or chyle from this digestion is intellectual development, as we see it in our skyscrapers, railways, works of art, and other products of the brain.

The dead or decayed races, nations, individuals are merely the excrement.

Civilized people are the food in the stomach today. Even as the food once placed in the mouth will normally pass through the alimentary canal in the form of chyle and waste, they too will pass.

Primitive peoples are the food of tomorrow. Some of these are peoples who have been through the process and are again ascending toward it, even as the dead body immediately again begins its ascent toward life.

The mixing of races is the variety in food.

The mixing of Negro with Caucasian is nature's getting at her reserve food. Food, rich with the accumulated sunshine and cheeriness of the ages, is being put into a pale, starving, intellectual body.

Racial intermixture is to the benefit of the Caucasian, and to the detriment of the Negro, even as the animal that is being eaten by another is the sufferer.

Another proof that racial intermixture is to the benefit of the Caucasian is that that race as we saw is more strongly attracted to the Negro than is the Negro to it.

The intellectual development of the Caucasian and its relation to the Negro is what a stimulant is to the stomach —not always wise to take.

How admirable, if cruel, is then the provision of Nature in regulating her food supply!

And how blurred the vision of those who disdain "races" not civilized like theirs!

Greedy, improvident fools! What, would you eat all at once?   R. H.

* * *

APPENDIX.

(1) For a long time the more developed of the European races, in spite of their far superior knowledge of methods for the preservation of life, have been declining through the mal-nutrition of Nature. This degeneracy, however, has been most noticeable within the past fifty years. Says Prof. W. Carmac Wilkinson: "The physical deterioration of the European races has been a subject of anxious

observation and inquiry of late years." This fact is perhaps most strikingly depicted in Beale's Racial Decay, wherein is to be found the opinions not of one man but of hundreds of the most learned Caucasian scholars from all parts of the world.

Says the Current Opinion of March, 1918:

"The most urgent demand of civilization at this hour is for population. . . .

The number of births in France like the number in England is diminishing with the constantly and precision of the regular parabola described by a stone falling to the earth. There were over a million births in 1876 and less than three-fourths of a million in 1913.

The war has accentuated every tendency to failing fertility in the white race of the western world.

The writer in the British Medical Journal proceeds:

" 'The birth rate, as is well known, has been falling pretty steadily for about half a century in all the countries of the western civilization but the fall began earlier in France than in the others and has been steadier.' "

According to report of the Hungarian Chamber of Deputies, January 13, 1918, the Hungarian birth-rate during the three years of war had decreased 50 per cent while the infant mortality had increased 50 per cent.

A similar condition prevails in all the warring countries.

According to Dr. Raymond Pearl, statistician of the U. S. Food Administration the net decrease in birth rate in 1917 was 48 per cent in Germany; 54 in Hungary; 24 in France, and 10 in England.

The Negro on his arrival to those shores, like the Indian, was free from syphilis and tuberculosis. Syphilis, mighty conqueror of the conquering Caucasian, dies in the African interior. Since the original Negro did not have syphilis or consumption it is evident it is the Caucasian who inoculated him.   R. H.

LETTER XXXIV.

My Dear Trent:

In your last letter I noticed that the sociologist says that according to my theory of racial intermixture there would then be no progress.

I will endeavor to answer this knotty, abstruse problem.

Now, in order to know whether there is progress it is essential that we first define progress. Is it what we call civilization? We saw, however, that civilization is destructive rather than constructive. Man in common parlance progresses or advances, but germs to eat him progress in numbers. Animals and savages have few diseases, civilized man many hundreds. Civilized man's entrance into the world is also more difficult. Birth pains increase. Pituitin, an aid to parturition, is unknown and unnecessary among savage women. The fear of death also increases. In China a man condemned to death may hire another to die for him, the money going to the man's family. Populations increase, but so does the killing greed of man, hence greater prisons, greater armies, bigger navies, bigger guns. Civilized man with his rapid-fire gun can kill thousands while the savage is killing one with his spear or boomerang. Increase knowledge and you decrease races and nations. Increase knowledge and you increase despondency; increase delicacy and you decrease resistance; increase refinement and you increase susceptibility to coarseness. Civilized man has the Fine Arts but he has also the loathsome Spirochete which gnaws off his limbs, and attacks him even in the third and fourth generation.

Progress, such as we deem it, is the lengthening of the memory of the human race, the unfolding of the intellect, the increasing imitation of Nature. We lengthen our historical records and call it progress.

But for blind, immutable Nature there can be no progress, as we understand that term, no more than one can ascribe progress to a clock at any time of its working. Everything in Nature is regulated with an awe-inspiring nicety. The earth and the other planets travel millions of miles every year around the sun, has been doing so for billions of years and is never a second behind time. Eclipses for hundred of years past or future can be accurately worked out.

Now if such fixity reigns outside of the earth, is it not safe to assume that the same laws reign within, the more so as we see that even as the earth revolves around its orbit, so the tiniest bit of earth known to man, the electron, is also revolving around its own infinitesimal orbit.

But an analysis of the different theories of a future life shows that most men have a mixed idea of what constitutes progress.

What does the white man hope will be the culmination of his busy life on earth? That he goes to heaven and for untold billions of years to do what? To loaf. The white man's idea of progress is nothing to do—and yet he accuses the Negro of being lazy.

The Indian believes he has fine hunting for evermore. Indian's idea of progress: good hunting.

The Turk's Paradise has an abundance of beautiful women. The Turk's idea of progress—sex enjoyment.

The Eskimo's idea of Heaven is a warm place. His heaven is our hell.

The white man with all his great trouble and worry is merely trying to get what Nature gives to the "savage" and still more so a tabby cat—ease from labor.

Progress, according to our optimistic notions of it could be made in only one way—the increase of pleasure and the decrease of pain. The idea of a Heaven proves this. But can the volume of pain be decreased? If it were possible for us to get rid of war and all pestilence and all crime would not pain yet be with us? We would have death, the thousand and one unavoidable accidents, shipwreck, storms, earthquakes, and what is far worse because war does not happen every day, is the thousand and one little irritations, the misunderstandings, and the pains of love. And what also of self-inflicted pain, the hundred needless fears with which we daily torment ourselves?

No, the balance must be kept. The measure of pain must keep pace with pleasure. Abolish pain in all its shades, and we have boredom, which brings us back to pain. Nothing to do is one of the most unbearable forms of pain. This, by the way, is why of all the hopes of a future existence, the white man's is the most simple-minded. If heaven is a painless place we will be bored if we retain our natures. If we do not it will do us no good as in order to appreciate pleasure we must experience pain. The stomach that never had to be fed would find no pleasure in food. Pleasure is satisfied need, and need is painful.

Progress is rather pain than pleasure; it means that we are being crunched in the digestive process of Nature.

There is no progress as we mortals usually imagine it. Animate Nature is a spark of the Infinite with the faculty of converting crude matter into various kinds of food, trees, fishes, horses, men and then consuming it. It is the babe with a spark of life that expands into a man from the food it has eaten.

Place that man on an island with a given supply of food, and no means of replenishing it, and he will eventually die of starvation. Likewise Earth, cut off from the other planets, as soon as her intellect has converted and consumed all the essence from crude matter, will die of starvation.

The human race, viewed as a single individual, is always hungry. The majority of humanity is half starved.

Many maintain that Nature is purposeless. The contrary is true. Nature, as confined to the solar system has a most definite purpose. That purpose is her own destruction. The life of the human individual, Nature at her highest, is emblematic of this.

Civilization is decay.

Progress is death.

Freedom from pain.

Oblivion.

R. H.

LETTER XXXV.

My Dear Trent:

Your letter received. "But if it is the purpose of Nature to use the Negro as a re-vitalizing force, why slavery; why cruel oppression," I notice, you object.

To explain:

That is merely an episode in the conflict of Nature. You see the individual thinks in only one direction, that which will give him pleasure. But what is one man's pleasure is the other fellow's gall. Victory is sweet to the conqueror, but bitter to the conquered. The death of your dearest loved one means money in the pocket of the undertaker. Slavery was sweet for the slaveholders, bitter for the slaves.

Pleasure and pain, or kindness and cruelty, are the component parts of Nature. Both demand satisfaction and racial intermixture is no exception to the rule. Lovers clearly destined for each other will meet the gravest opposition from parents. "The course of true love never did run smooth."

To further explain the nature of this conflict as we see it in the mixing of Negro and Caucasian:

The white man, an evolution of primitive man far more likely than not of some Negro race, has attained great development. That is one side.

You may remember what I said of the necessity of Nature to return to primitive conditions, in other words, to take in a fresh supply while the civilized peoples are being digested. That is the other side.

Now, the whites, already in a state of digestion, object to new food—the Negro—being put in the same stomach with them. But the stomach must have it or it will soon go empty. Hence, the battle between the white man, and the stomach or Nature.

But the white man is only a part of Nature—he is in the stomach and all he can ever do is to make a fuss—hence, while he objects with his mouth or intellect, the stomach of Nature bends him to it. Result, the gross sexual immorality that now prevails.

Tennyson, in Locksley Hall, has strikingly expressed this antagonism in racial intermixture. Here speaks the heart, voice of mother Nature:

> "There the passions cramped no longer shall have
> scope and breathing space.
> I will take some savage woman she shall rear
> my dusky race.
>
> Iron jointed, supple sinewed, they shall dive and
> they shall run
> Catch the wild goat by the hair and hurl their
> lances in the sun.
>
> Whistle back the parrot's call, and leap the
> rainbows of the brooks,
> Not with blinded eyesight poring over miser-
> erable books.

But now speaks second nature, intellectual development or Pride, one and the same with the spirit that made the judge in another famous poem to refuse Maud Muller when

> "He thought of his sisters proud and cold, and
> his mother vain of her rank and gold,"

one and the same with the spirit that makes the poor girl to give up her strong and youthful lover, the one for whom her heart yearns, to marry some rich man of strong social position. Says second nature as voiced by Tennyson:

> "I, to herd with narrow foreheads vacant of our
> glorious gains,
> Like a beast with lower pleasures, like a beast
> with lower pains.
>
> "I, the heir of all the ages, in the foremost files
> of times,
> Match with a squalid savage what to me were
> time or tide?"

This desire to return to the primitive is also voiced in Beaumont and Fletcher's "Philaster," act IV, scene II:

> 'Oh that I had been nourished in these woods,
> And then had taken me some mountain girl,
> Beaten with winds, chaste as the hardened rocks
> Whereon she dwells, that might have strewed my
>   bed
> With leaves and reeds and with the skins of
>   beasts,
> Our neighbors, and have borne at her big breasts
> My large, coarse issue."

Distaste of certain whites to mating with Negroes is merely the regulator of variety in Nature's human food supply and differs only in degree from the individual's distaste for certain foods—a distaste largely due to custom. Love is merely nutrition in another form. Very affectionate lovers will speak of eating one another, and then there is cunnilinguis. The mother will often affectionately bite her infant.

Our distaste for mating with individuals of another "race" is merely a heightened form of that dislike for mating with certain of our own. Both forms are necessary. Race prejudice, on the other hand, is the distaste for mating, plus badness of heart.

EPIPHILOSOPHY.

Faust. "I've now alas!   Philosophy
Medicine and Jurisprudence, too;
And to my cost, Theology,
With ardent labor studied through,
And here I stand with all my lore,
Poor fool, no wiser than before."

And in this mixing of races, which is right, the wisdom of Nature or the wisdom of man?

Billions of years before this earth was spun from nebulous matter, millions of years before man acquired an intellect, Nature was at work. It is only within the past fifty years or so that man has sufficiently loosened the grip of theology and superstition on his throat, and is having an opportunity to learn something about his body, and its relation to Nature, and this knowledge at its very highest is now rudimentary. We know how prone the human intellect is to err, how little able to distinguish the true from the false. A conspicuous example was the premature peace celebration all over the world. I never see a blind man go tapping, tapping along the street to find the way than I think of the human race, in its search for knowledge.

One of the most instructive object lessons in the fallibility of the mind, its almost incredible imperfections are the facts presented in Andrew D. White's "Warfare Between Science and Theology in Christendom," to see how tenaciously the most absurd beliefs, beliefs so ridiculous that few today, however ignorant, would credit them were held and fought for by the wisest and ablest of the time; even to the perpetration of the most horrible cruelties. The more I think, the firmer grows the conviction that the intellect was evolved for receiving impressions just strong enough to take care of the body, for no other thought but of nourishment and sex, or how else could it accommodate itself so easily to beliefs, especially those that the individual wishes to be true. The young intellect accommodates itself to belief as water to a mold. The more simple-minded the man the more incisive his beliefs. Why? Because his weak intellect limits his theories to a few, possibly to one, and he has no other against which to match it. Persons of this

type who are ardent Christians in Europe would be just as
ardent Mohammedans had they been reared in Turkey. It is
safe to say that had the American slave holders been Buddhists that the Negroes of the New World would have been
as ardent Buddhists as they are now Christians.

A few illustrations to show the infantile nature of the
intellect in even the wisest: Pliny, the greatest scholar of
his day, tells us in his Natural History that hailstones and
even lightning will be scared away by a woman uncovering
herself at menstrual periods during a storm, and also that
if a woman walks in this state through a field of corn, all
caterpillars, worms, beetles, and other vermin will fall from
the ears of corn. This, by the way, the Cappodocian wom-
en used to do. Further on he says of the Greeks: "There is
no falsehood if ever so barefaced, to which some of them
cannot be found to bear testimony," and then goes right on to
say himself: "Another thing universally acknowledged and
one which I am ready to believe with the greatest pleasure
is the fact that if the door posts are only touched with the
menstrous fluid all the spells of the magician will be neut-
ralized."

The Romans believed that a rooster once spoke to a
man, and the Jews that a donkey did, a belief still held by
many graduates of universities today. Galen and Hippoc-
rates, leading physicians of their day, believed in the effi-
cacy or fatality of the number seven. "For countless years,"
writes Dr. Victor Robinson, "the Augean stables of the
materia medica were indiscriminately emptied into the human alimentary canal, weakening and poisoning unlimited
hordes of men, women and children."

Bacon, the wisest man of his day, held beliefs that a
modern school boy would laugh to scorn; many whites of the
best classes have a deadly fear of Fridays and the number
13. Large numbers of educated whites would never occupy
the thirteenth berth on a sleeping car; and, according to the
newspapers, Bishop Fallows of Chicago telegraphed President
Wilson that he thought it a psychological error to have to
have draft registration day on a Friday.

And rich as the efflorescence of ignorance and obstinacy
has been in theology or other fields, far richer, has it been
in the doctrine of Negro inferiority. An instructive mirror

for those who still maintain Negro inferiority is to read some of the stuff put out by their predecessors and as late as twenty or even ten years ago, as "The Negro," by Ariel; "Negro-Mania," by Campbell; "Slavery," by Josiah Priest; "The Six Species of Man," by the Anti-Abolition Society, and "The Color Line," by W. B. Smith. The sole difference between these types is that one is an up-to-date version of the other, that one tried to do with Hebrew mythology what the other is trying to do with a smattering of science—a smattering consisting largely of pompous, bewildering terminology. When I consider the proneness of the mind to belief, especially to such as flatter, I cannot but think what a dangerous thing it is that men like "Putnam Weale" and Schultz, for instance, should be able to get hold of this pseudo-science of Ethnology. It is as dangerous as giving a loaded pistol to a three-year-old baby.

Mankind, today, is heading toward two great camps, colored and white, and if they ever come to a clash, which in all probability they will, Anthropology and Ethnology, as supported by Theology, and interpreted by the Caucasian will be the criminals. The doctrine of superiority of the Germans over the rest of the Caucasian race as sown by Gobineau, and watered by Chamberlain and others was the incentive to Prussian Kultur.

But the true man of science will recognize this fact; the doctrine of evolution, and of the survival of the fittest, Mendel's law, Weissman's theory and other scientific postulates have been deduced from Nature and not Nature from them. They function, if at all, according to Nature and not Nature them. Man is already here, an accomplished fact and the best that any scientist can do is to endeavor to explain how he got here. And the truth is that it seems to matter little whether the scientist explains man or not, for the more he explains, the more he has to explain. At present we have a number of facts, and are merely piecing them together hoping to settle the problems posed by the mind. Mankind continues to exist, not because of, but in spite of doctors and eugenists.

Science while indispensable for putting civilized humanity back on the paths from which it has wandered through its defective mentality must function with feeling, must ever be inspired by the kind heart, must have as its patron saint, Christ rather than Nietzche.

If Science does not make man kindlier to man then it is a cruel snare. Life is sensation of pleasure and pain, therefore kindness of heart is of infinitely greater import than all the wisdom of science.

There is talk of the Negro's lowering intellectual standards but were it even so, could we not get along with less intellect, and more gentleness, more humanity? The Negro is by nature far gentler than the Caucasian whose life has been a constant assertion of the will, a selfish looking after himself, and the Negro's gentler nature will go toward rendering it more humane. Who does not wish that Germany had a little less head, and a little more heart? Germany, where literacy is much higher than in any other country. The most intellectual of all peoples, and the most brutal. Brutal even to her own. According to Klinast the authorities rejoiced that in 1917, 720,000 more persons between the ages of fifty and seventy-five died than in 1914, because it made so many more unproductive mouths to feed. The most dangerous, the most pernicious, cruel and heartless thing in the world is intellect, unaccompanied by high moral principles. That is the lesson Germany has taught the world to its bitter cost.

And will the world learn the lesson, especially the leading Caucasian nations? for the attitude of Great Britain and the United States, foremost oppressors of the darker races, differs not a whit from the attitude of Germany to the rest of the Caucasian race. The difference between the Kultur of Prussia and the Jim-Crowism of America lies solely in the difference of the beam that is in one man's eye and the mote in another. And you may depend upon it that just as the forces of Right arose and swept the German Empire into oblivion, even so will those forces again arise to obliterate oppressive nations.

I feel that I value as much as any other the blessings of civilization, but I cannot lose sight of the fact that it is more destructive than constructive. The more advanced Caucasian groups are like a horde of wolves in the chase, the members of which will immediately stop and rend any of the pack that shows signs of weakening—cold, heartless, cruel, grasping.

What deluges of woe has not the white man visited upon the darker peoples? What mountains of crime and cruelty mark his pathway over the earth! The Indian exterminated or herded into corners; the Australian and Tasmanian relentlessly butchered; India scourged and plundered in the name of God; China cheated; the Eskimo pilfered; Africa, hospitable Africa, robbed, raped, maimed, her children killed for sport, or thrown to the sharks. Brutality, Brutality, unrealisable Brutality! For every ounce of good that the white man's culture or religion has done to the darker races, it has done a ton of harm.

"How the European has been able to establish Colonies," says Nietzche, "is explained by his nature which is that of a beast of prey."

But the superman will never be the happy man. Tenderhearted Nietzche's own life forecasts the doom of his superman. To live beyond good and evil is to be evil. If superman there be he must be a man pre-eminently kind. The more advanced of the Caucasian groups are living according to Nietzche's formula, that is why they are the unhappiest of all peoples.

* * *

With regard to the superior wisdom of Nature, Havelock Ellis, apparently the foremost authority on matters of sex, says:

"The wisdom of man working through a few centuries or in one corner of the earth, by no means necessarily corresponds to the wisdom of Nature, and may be in flat opposition to it. This is especially the case when the wisdom of man merely means, as sometimes happens, the experience of our ancestors gained under other conditions or merely the opinions of one class or sex. Taking a broad view of the matter, it seems difficult to avoid the conclusion that it is safer to trust to the conservatism of Nature than the conservatism of Man."

For example, what would happen if man had the controlling voice in the determination of sex? Male infants, the lesser necessity, are most in demand and in parts of China, and India, girl babies are considered hardly human, being drowned like kittens or puppies.

But what of the mixing of defectives? Is not Nature responsible for that? one might ask.

The defective is a product of civilization and is continued by civilization. Among savages and animals the weak die off in the struggle for existence. Civilization builds almshouses, asylums, etc., to perpetuate them. There is, however, no relevancy between the mixing of races and the marriage of defectives.

* * *

Anti-marriage laws are a reflection of the gross stupidity of those who make them. But we ought to expect no better when one considers that it is chiefly the sharper or shyster lawyer, men whose mission it is to prove that "fair is foul and foul is fair" who control the political situation in the South.

Racial intermixture is a cosmic force. Just as the etiolated plant in the cellar stretches toward the sunlight so the Caucasian, etiolated man, yearns for the pent-up sunlight in the black. It is one and the same law of Nature, for as Professor Moulton so profoundly summarizes it, we are blossoms of the sun.

Color in this respect is more profoundly significant than mankind is aware of.

* * *

Laws against intermarriage are as old as humanity. Most primitive peoples have them. In Biblical times the Jews forbade intermarriage, reserving, however, the right to take the virgins captured in war. We find the infatuated Ezra tearing his garments and his beard that the "holy seed" should marry with Gentile nations.

But these laws had little effect—Moses the maker of the law breaking it by marrying a Negro woman. Gentiles in many European and Asiatic countries are today giving the Jews a dose of their own medicine, also with no better results. In ancient Rome there were severe laws against the marriage of patrician and the rural plebs, also with little effect. This law was finally adjudged unconstitutional and unjust and the Canuleian law was passed giving Roman citizens the right to marry whom they pleased.

During the religious wars of the Middle Ages there were also laws forbidding the marriage of Catholic and Protestant and as late as the 18th Century priests who performed such ceremonies were put to death.

To illustrate the monstrous stupidity and gross injustice of anti-marriage laws, its utter heartlessness: It is well known that men do not usually try to seduce young women in their own class. They go to a lower one. Now let us suppose it possible to keep every Negro woman always on a level below the whites, debase them if you will. Would that keep away the white man with his cosmic urge? I have seen white men when they cannot get better ones, with colored women that I shudder from.

And would it leave the white wife untouched, and finally the whole nation?

But to question further. If the objection is the marriage of the white woman to the black man even here Nature can be trusted. The present attitude is not only not complimentary to the white woman, but an insult. It assumes that a white woman if left unwatched would fly at the first black man she met, it assumes that a marriage had all been arranged for some white man's daughter or sister regardless of taste, to marry a promiscuous black man and but for the providential interposition of the objector would have taken place. And if the white woman would so act toward Negroes whom she is not supposed to like what must her attitude be toward white men whom she is supposed to like?

But so-called white women are not so indiscriminate in their loves as certain white men would have us infer. Woman is, on the whole, far more discriminating than man, for as Ward so aptly puts it while Nature says to man: Fecundate, she says to the woman: Discriminate. Kafir women, says Dudley Kidd, are very discriminating. The men go scantily clad, and those with any bodily defects or ugly scars have a poor chance of getting a wife. With most men gratification is the principal thing; with most women, a tertiary one. The sexual urge is greater in man, for while the number of germs produced by one man in his life runs into the trillions, those by woman only into the thousands. The normal woman seeks maternity and very many highly cultured maids often wish there were other means of becoming mothers than by Nature's process.

It is true that women are often influenced by wealth, flattery and social position yet such often pay dearly for it, for love and tenderness is infinitely more important to them, and they are never content without it.

* * *

The treatment of this question belongs to the realm of the genius rather than that of the scientist. I do not think we will ever be able to grasp life in the manner the scientists are attempting, to be able to seize upon it and say, "It is this, as one would the superficies of an apple. The more one ponders life, the more bewildered he becomes. Who is there can answer the question: "What am I?" This is because life is feeling, sensation of pleasure and pain, and there is nothing in common between the properties of intellect and the properties of feeling. It takes like to comprehend like, thus feeling to comprehend feeling.

And with feeling, the genius is endowed immeasurably beyond the ordinary man. Genius is really an extraordinary, an exquisitely attuned sense for receiving impressions. Genius is super-sensitivity. The genius sees a thousand beauties of form and color where the ordinary man would see none, is enraptured by the magical coloring on the wing of a fly or the poetic grace of a flower. He feels a thousand pangs at rudeness and clumsiness where the ordinary man would feel none. He has, too, an exquisitely fine sense of what is just and sees rudeness and injustice where the ordinary man sees none. He is above everything else kind-hearted, a man of infinite tenderness, the All-Mother at her tenderest—for Nature is really more kind than cruel. Were Nature more cruel than kind, life could not exist. The genius is kind-hearted and we find Cowper saying that he would never count among his friends any one who would willingly crush a worm. The difference between the genius and the ordinary man may be likened to the difference between the reaction of a nerve in a broken tooth, and that of one in a sound tooth. This acuteness of feeling puts him in connection with the whole universe. His nervous system is in direct connection with the great nerves of Nature.

On the other hand, the anthropologist, the morphologist, the histologist and the doctors of heredity unless they blend philosophy with their knowledge can never be other than superficial—mere analyzers of the mechanism of Nature. While the genius pierces the depths, the scientist glides on the surface; the difference between the deep sea diver and the swimmer, between the chemist who takes up a glass of sea water to analyze it and the oceanographer who sends his rod far, far into the depths to sound the floor of the ocean. Life is feeling, sensation of pleasure and pain and the problems of life must be solved by feeling. And kindly feeling because it is that which we one and all prefer.

* * *

Three of the world's greatest geniuses, Shakespeare, Maupassant and Victor Hugo, have treated this matter of union of Negro and Caucasian from the standpoint of feeling and have shown that it is in perfect accord with Nature. In Othello we see that while Brabantio thought it abnormal that the lovely Desdemona should leave the wealthy curled darlings of Venice to marry Othello, yet to the lovers themselves their love was the most natural thing in the world. That Othello did murder her was due to the perfidy and jealousy of the white Iago.

Shakespeare has further given us in Titus Andronicus that of which so much exists in the United States, the illicit love of a white woman for a black man, that of the beautiful Queen Tamora, for the black Aaron.

Maupassant in Boitelle touchingly depicts how the life of a white man was completely ruined because his parents objected to the girl he so tenderly loved because they thought her too black. In Hugo's "Bug Jargal," we find the black man grieving for the white woman. These geniuses have, as I said, shown that love between black and white is quite natural.

Finally Sir H. H. Johnston who possesses the irresistible combination of a great heart and a great head points out:

"Those few scientific men of Britain, Germany, France, the United States and Brazil, who have striven to understand the anthropology of the Negro and to compare it with the white man are inclined rather than otherwise to argue now that the Negro and the Negroid have contributed in the past, and still more may contribute in the future a very important quota to the whole sum of humanity, an element of soundness and stability in physical development and certain mental qualities which the perfected man of, let us say, twenty-two or twenty-three centuries after Christ cannot afford to do without."

Moreover this is not the first time within the memory of man that intermixture between black and white has taken place perhaps as proportionately great as that now taking place in the United States. As late as the Norman Conquest (1066) a considerable portion of the people of Great Britain and Ireland, and especially of Scotland was black as set forth in "Ancient and Modern Britons"—a truth, which flatly contradicts William Archer when he says in his rather biased book, "Through Afro-America," "Our deepest instincts inherited through a thousand generations."

The European is a mixture of African Negro, Hottentot, Mongolian, African and Australian Bushman and some other Asiatic, probably the Hindu. To quote from "Ancient and Modern Britons:"

"So far as complexion goes there can be no doubt as to the presence of a vast infusion of "colored" blood. There are, of course, no living Britons who are as black as Negroes, but some are as dark as mulattoes, and many darker than Chinamen. To regard ourselves, in the mass, as 'white people' except in a comparative degree, is quite a mistake.

"This varied ancestry connects us with almost every nation under the sun—we have inherited the blood that is akin to that of many savage races now alive."

Sir H. H. Johnston at the Universal Races Congress said:

"Recent discoveries made in the vicinity of the principality of Monaco, and others in Italy and Western France—all of them analysed in monograph on the skulls found in the grottoes of Grimaldi edited by Dr. Verneaux, of Paris, and published in 1909 by the Prince of Monaco—would seem to reveal even if some of their deductions are discounted and a few statements regarded as erroneous, the actual fact that many thousand years ago a negroid race had penetrated through Italy into France leaving traces at the present day in the physiognomy of the peoples of Southern Italy, Sicily,

Sardinia, Southern and Western France and even in the western parts of the United Kingdom of Great Britain and Ireland. There are even at the present day some examples of the Keltiberian peoples of Western Scotland, Southern and Western Wales, Southern and Western Ireland of distinctly Negroid aspect, and in whose ancestry there is no indication whatever of any connection with the West Indies or with modern Africa. Still more marked is this feature in the peoples of Southern and Western France and of other parts of the Mediterranean already mentioned."

Sir Arthur Evans, president of the British Association for the Advancement of Science said in his 1916 address: "One must never lose sight of the fact that from the earliest Aurignacian period onwards a Negroid element in the broadest sense of the term shared in this artistic culture as seen on both sides of the Pyrenees."

All of this is quite apart from the fact that for the past five thousand years or so intermarriage has uninterruptedly gone on between black and white on both shores of the Mediterranean. Our Italian population has a considerable infusion of Negro blood.

* * *

Will intermarriage solve the race problem is the question often asked. Has it solved it, is the more fitting one. Up to the present the whites have shown little restraint and would the pronouncing of a few words by preacher or clerk have softened the situation for the mulatto? Children of legally married mixed couples have just as hard a time.

That the question of intermarriage—the fear of racial intermixture—although it seems to loom so large in the thought of the whites actually enters little, if at all, into the racial situation, I shall attempt to prove:

So far as attitude toward the Negro goes, the whites may be divided into two groups, those who are repelled ostensibly on account of "race" and those who are attracted because of, and in spite of it.

Now, let us suppose the Negro was as wealthy as the whites. Those who do not like him, would treat with him, because of his money, even as those who do not like Jews, treat with them. We make friends quickly with those from whom there is a chance of getting something. A small favor or present will often alter our entire view with regard to a person. It is the rare man who will permit racial, religious, political or even ethical scruples to stand in the way of his making money. The basis, the real, the burning question of life is money or its equivalent. As the man without intellect decries intellect, so the man without money decries money, but the fact remains that money is the greatest, most tremendous force in life. Everything else but the inevitable goes down before it. The difference between the man who has money, and the one who has not, is almost as great as the difference between the living and the dead.

And this nigh omnipotent force works with equal impartiality, for all who possess it. A wealthy Negro certainly looks bigger to the whole world than a poor white man. The Negro is disliked or belittled not because of his color but because of his poverty. Poor whites are also slighted or ignored but the Negro suffers more because in addition he wears a badge of color.

Money, not intermarriage, is the real issue in the racial situation.

Again with his easy-going ways and lovable, cheerful disposition, the Negro would soon win the hearts of those who at first merely tolerated him for his money.

With the whites of the second group, there would of course be no trouble. What is holding these from recognizing the Negro is also lack of money. The Negro is, in this respect, like a poor girl in the power of a dishonorable lover. But let that girl suddenly acquire, say wealth, and a title, see how quickly he would wish to marry her.

It is true that there are Negroes of wealth and position but these are so few as to be almost if not quite obscured.

Intermarriage will not solve the problem. The two races could go on mixing for the next hundred years, and if the Negroes remained poor they would still be no better off. The fewer rich always dominate the greater poor. When legally and socially approved intermarriages take place the question will already have been solved.

Besides marriage with its many misunderstandings is often a creator of problems.

"Intermarriage" is a bugaboo. It is one of those fears with which we pester ourselves for a long time, only to find out that we have been tormenting ourselves unnecessarily. Perfectly natural, like anything else seen through a mist, it frightens persons who do not think for themselves.

Intermarriage is a slogan, probably having its beginning with the "democratic" party in 1860. It is a slogan given to the masses by the politicians, employers of labor, and all who make money out of the Negro's predicament. Schemers use intermarriage to frighten the grown white babies as mothers use bogies to frighten the little ones.

To talk of intermarriage as a solution is to put the cart before the horse. Money is the thing. Iago's reiterated advice to Roderigo, "Put money in thy purse," should be the slogan of Negro leaders.

* * *

Another much talked of solution is classical education. The advocates of this are even more short-sighted, for, let us suppose, by way of the impossible, that every Negro had the ability of absorbing a classical education. What could he do without money? The whites are highly egotistic, and the easiest thing in the world is to discount learning in others. It takes knowledge, and the most sublime form of knowledge to discern that another is better informed than one's self. Illiterate persons are the most obstinately certain that they are right.

Moreover, learning is at a discount in the United States. Perhaps of all the Caucasian countries, Russia and the United States place the least value upon intellectual ability, the former because of its great illiteracy, the latter, because of its commercial spirit, and worship of gold.

One thing is sure, the intellectual Negro might expect little recognition from the whites with their Bolsheviki attitude towards learning so far as Negroes are concerned, and hardly any more from his own people. Intellectual development increases one's desires, and for the poor Negro it is like taking an appetizer preparatory to sitting down to a Barmecide feast.

Development through industrial channels is undoubtedly the Negro's easiest way of coming into his own. It is a wise father who sees that his son or daughter, however gifted, has a trade.

But this will take time, a long time, and the demand of the suffering as always is instant relief. There is, so far as I can see, but one way of accomplishing this; the dropping of the lower class white man, by the cultivated classes, thus permitting the adoption of those principles of civic conduct so admirably defined in the Constitution of the United States, and the Declaration of Independence—principles, which, to-day, so far as color is concerned, are more honored in the breach than in the observance.

But here is another obstacle. Who in this respect constitutes the cultivated class? Take a banking institution. Is it not the better class of whites who would be supposed to work in such a place? Yet the majority would protest the employment of a colored person, however refiined or talented, except as porter or maid. Or again in certain colleges? The truth is, it is the better and the best classes of whites who are at the bottom of the trouble. The lyncher and the rioter are in relation to the better class of whites merely what the hand is to the brain. The sole difference between a lyncher and Thomas Dixon, for instance, is that their differing talents cause their common dislike to differently express itself—one with the torch, the other with the pen.

Howbeit the low-class white man cuts a most ridiculous figure in the eyes of the thinking Negro. The trumpetings of superiority on his behalf serves but to accentuate his horrible limitations.

Plutarch said that the placing of an insignificant man on a pedestal served but to magnify his littleness. The lower class white man is at present on a pedestal side by side with the more efficient classes. From this height he looks arrogantly down on his betters among the colored people. But his pedestal is an inflated bladder and needs only a pin-prick to bring the imposter back to earth.

His condition though is really an asset to the Negro, for as long as the low-class whites are led to believe that they are the equal of the better class whites, and the superior of talented Negroes, they will be content with that froth.

A sense of inherited superiority is the greatest of all handicaps.

So far as amalgamation is concerned, I would very much rather that we as a group be left to develop ourselves without any further infusion of Caucasian blood. It is almost certain that we have nothing to gain by intermixture, that we would not develop by fair treatment.

If we are decadent it is clear that we can gain nothing by mixing with a people who, according to their own confession, are already in the advanced stages of decay. If, for instance, as Davenport tells us, that the mulatto has worse teeth than the full-blooded Negro,—a fact—it is clear that since he must have inherited this defect somewhere he got it from his Caucasian parent, who, in that case, must have had still worse teeth. If the mulatto is not so hardy as the black, it is clear that the Caucasian is still less hardy. If one kind of wine is good, and after mixing it with another, we get an inferior product, it is certain that the second kind is worse than the mixture. My most honest conviction is that we have nothing to gain, physically, spiritually or intellectually by an infusion of Caucasian blood. Whatever disease we may have acquired either through intermixture or by hard-living conditioins would, under fair treatment gradually be compensated for and expunged by the great vitality of the full blood Negro.

* * *

And as regards the future of the Negro?

Lester F. Ward in his "Applied Sociology," furnishes a picture, I think most prophetic of the relation between the Negro "proletariat" and the Caucasian "aristocrat" in the South—relations which are slowly but surely being reversed.

"The history of social classes," he says, "furnishes to the philosophical student of society, the most convincing proof that the lower grades of mankind have never occupied those positions on account of any inherent incapacity to occupy higher ones. Throughout antiquity and well down through the Middle Ages, the great mass of mankind were slaves. A little later they were serfs bound to the soil. Finally with the abolition of slavery, the fall of the feudal system and the establishment of the industrial system, this great mass took the form of a proletariat, the fourth estate, considered of so little consequence that they are seldom mentioned by the great historians of Europe. Even at the close of the eighteenth century when the greatest of all political revolutions occurred it was only the third estate that was at all in evidence—the business class, bourgeoisie, or social mesoderm. This class had been looked down upon and considered inferior and only the lords spiritual and temporal were regarded as capable of controlling social and national affairs. This class is now at the top. It has furnished the world's brains for two centuries, and if there is any intellectual inferiority, it is to be found in the poor remnant that stills calls itself the nobility in some countries."

It is impossible to keep down the Africans of America, as impossible as preventing the flow of a river by damning it. If hardship and brutality could have done so they would have vanished like the Indians of the West Indies. The Bantus say, "The Negro race is like a rubber ball, the harder you throw it down, the higher it rises."

And this is no rhetoric.

At present the Africans of America do not know themselves, do not realise the incisive quality of their latent power. They cater to the white man, they look at themselves through his eyes, their sunny, forgiving natures permit them to be deceived, but some day they are really going to think for themselves, and when they do, they are going to rise to a point where they will be stronger and more aggressive than if they had been fairly treated. Misfortune crushes the weak man, the strong man deliberately seizes it and therewith builds a ladder rising transcendent above his fellows. It is the nature of the Negro to progress, even as it is that of hydrogen to rise above the surrounding atmosphere. Today, in many a university, many a position, the Negro youth has outstripped his white fellows simply because he felt it incumbent to do something to offset the stigma placed on his color.

The good name and all the democratic pretensions of the United States are quite at stake in this matter of Negro treatment, for as long as a cultured and refined man who is "colored" is restrained by law from coming and going with the freedom of an ex-convict, who is "white," then our pretensions to democracy is a brutal and barefaced humbug; as long as color distinctions continue the upholders of the dignified Constitution of the United States are confederates of the miserable Jim-Crow laws of the Southern States; as long as human beings continue to be burnt alive on the altar of the God, Racial Superiority, so long will the statue of Liberty, torch in hand, be peculiarly reminiscent of the lyncher, and as long as talent, refinement, and education are depreciated in citizens because of color, so long will the Caucasians of the United States be not unlike that other portion of their race—the uncouth, purblind, illiterate, much to be pitied, Bolsheviki of Russia.

While every group has a perfect right to keep itself to itself, to entirely control its own affairs, to say where it will and where it will not marry, yet the instant it enters the life of another group, so surely does it forfeit that right, and the other group has now a right to reciprocally interfere. It is clear that in the beginning the black man wished no association with the white, and that the white has all along forced his company upon him. If the white man will not leave the Negro alone, but wishes to mix with him, the Negro has a perfect right, that is, if justice is to prevail, to say under what conditions that mixing shall take place.

It is evident that the irritation proceeds rather from the Caucasian, therefore, it is his duty to take the forward steps in adjustment, in short, it would be well to bear in mind that we have not so much a Negro problem as a Caucasian one.

For my part, I earnestly desire a kindly and unqualified justice for every citizen regardless of color or sex. The trend of events points to the welding into one of this heterogenous mass, we call America, and it is the bounden duty of every lover of his country to see that that process be accomplished with the least rancor, and the greatest degree of high-mindedness.

The color line bestializes. It forces human beings to meet on a plane where the barriers of decency are already broken down.

A developed Negro means a richer United States.

An oppressed Negro means not only a weaker United States but a weaker Caucasian race.

The unvarnished truth is that in this treatment of the Negro, the whites, and I have in mind the majority of most of the cultivated classes, are not observing the first principles of politeness, of that good breeding and courtesy to all, which the wisest, best and noblest of their race for the past three thousand years have unweariedly taught.

Does our cause, be it racial, religious or political, render us inconsiderate of the rights of others? Then it is wrong and sure to fail.

Every Caucasian who stands against Negro development is an enemy of his country, and the principles for which it stands.

Down with the Dixons, Hoke Smiths, Bleases, Heflins, Hardwicks, John Sharp Williams, and all those others who would waken or encourage the beast in the best of us. Down with all those who would deliberately fatten on the miseries of others. Such men in high life, in lowly life, would rob, slay, burn; would pillage the dead.

What are the agencies employed to maintain the color line? Murder, foulest murder; hate; arson; theft; deceit; concubinage. I challange anyone to name a single honorable quality

These are the guardians of white supremacy; I repeat them: Murder, Hate, Arson, Theft, Deceit, Concubinage.

Christ or Barabbas?

Barabbas, the thief, the robber of the rights of his fellow-citizens; or Christ, the honest.

The honor, dignity and happiness, not only of the nation, but of our individual selves demand a cessation of this injustice.

> "United States! the ages plead,
>   Present and past in under-song,
> Go put your creed into your deed,
>   Nor speak with double tongue.
>
> Be just at home; then write your scroll,
>   Of honor o'er the sea,
> And bid the broad Atlantic roll,
>   A ferry of the free.
>
> For He that worketh high and wise,
>   Nor pauses in his plan,
> Will take the sun out of the skies,
>   Ere freedom out of man."
>
>   —Emerson.

THE END.

As Nature Leads

ISBN 13: 978-0-933121-15-7
ISBN 10: 0-933121-15-6

Printed by BCP Digital Printing, Inc.,
an affiliate company of Black Classic Press

Founded in 1978, Black Classic Press specializes in bringing to ligh
obscure and significant works by and about people of African descent. If ou
books are not available in your area, ask your local bookseller to order them.

Visit www.blackclassicbooks.com for a full list of our titles

You may also obtain a list of our current tiles by writing to:
Black Classic Press
c/o List
P.O. Box 13414
Baltimore, MD 21203

CORRIGENDA

Page	Para.	Line		
9	8	4	Read	"how explain"
26	2	9	"	"to understand more clearly"
26	2	10	"	"even to publish"
28	3	1	"	"Coloured" for "Colored"
61	1	6	"	"the greater part" for "majority"
68	5	8	"	add "The most appaling thing to me was the
		5		number of young white boys and girls I found
				mixing with colored people. (Chicago Herald,
				Nov. 16, 1917, speaking of one of these Cabarets")
				"Coloured" for "Colored"
70	2		"	"A white one" for "white one"
80	4		"	"coloring" for "colorings"
81	last line		"	"increase" for "increases"
93	2	5	"	delete "the" after "made"
99	4	11	"	"Coloured" for "Colored"
108	10	1	"	"related" for "such as happened"
112	1	11	"	"place" in quotation marks
128	3	6	"	"works of its kind" for "works"
131	2	5	"	"eighty-six" for "eighty & six tenths"
134	3	3	"	"pseudo-scientific" for "scientific"
136	3	4	"	"arithmetical" for "arithmetic"
138	3	3	"	"bubble" for "bubbles"
140	2	5	"	"is now baffled"
140	3	1	"	"Result of this discontent: awakening"
143	7	4	"	"On" for "about"
167	4	5	"	after "world" add "and its transmission by
				intermixture"
170	3	2	"	at bottom add "END OF LETTERS"
189			"	after "principal" add "reason for mar-
196	5	9		riage"
205	5	6	"	"are" for "is"

A Select List of Black Classic Press Titles

The Negro
W. E. B. DuBois

Originally published in 1915, Dr. W. E. Burghardt Du Bois' "little book," as h
called it, was one of the most important and seminal works on African and Africa
American history. It was small in size but gigantic in purpose. In it Du Boi:
unquestionably an eminent historian, brilliantly attempted to encapsulate the te
thousand-year record of the peoples of Africa, then referred to as "Negroes."
Introduction by W. Burghardt Turner and Joyce Moore Turner.
ISBN 1-58073-032-9. 1915*, 2005. 281 pp. Paper $14.95.

David Walker's Appeal
David Walker

Walker's Appeal represents one of the earliest African-centered discourses on an
oppressed people's right to freedom. African American political philosophy has
evolved from many of the themes that it articulates.
ISBN 0-933121-38-5. 1929*, 1993. 108 pp. Paper $8.95.

A Tropical Dependency
Flora Shaw Lugard

When Lady Lugard sat down to write *A Tropical Dependency*, it was not he
intention to inspire generations of Africans to regain the independence of the
countries. Lugard writes of slavery as though it was a God-given right c
Europeans to own Africans as slaves. Ironically, her text on Africa's place i
history reaffirms the belief that "If Africa did it once, Africa can do it again!"
Introduction by John Henrik Clarke.
ISBN 0-933121-92-X. 1906*, 1997. 508 pp. Paper $24.95.

The Name "Negro": Its Origin and Evil Use
Richard B. Moore

Moore's study focuses on the exploitive nature of the word "Negro." Connectin
its origins to the African Slave Trade, he shows how the label "Negro" was used t
separate African descendants and to confirm their supposed inferiority.
ISBN 0-933121-35-0. 1960*, 1992. 108 pp. Paper $10.95.

Wonderful Ethiopians of the Ancient Cushite Empire
Drusilla Dunjee Houston

Mrs. Houston describes the origin of civilization and establishes links among th
ancient Black populations of Arabia, Persia, Babylonia, and India. In each cas
she concludes that the ancient Blacks who inhabited these areas were all cultural
related.
ISBN 0-933121-01-6. 1926*, 1985. 280 pp. Paper $14.95.

The Exiles of Florida
Joshua R. Giddings

uring the early part of the nineteenth century, the United States conducted a brutal
ampaign to re-enslave Blacks who escaped slavery and found freedom in Native
merican settlements in Florida. Giddings' observations document the struggle
aged by these brave Africans and their Native American hosts.
;BN 0-933121-47-4. 1858*, 1997. 338 pp. Paper $16.95.

Ancient Egypt the Light of the World
Gerald Massey

n epic analysis of ancient origins and beliefs, this first volume of Ancient Egypt
aborates how the first humans, who emerged in Africa, created thought. In the
cond volume Massey examines the Precession of the Equinoxes and the old
amite sources of Christianity.
BN 0-933121-31-8. 1907*, 1992. 944 pp. Paper $59.95.

A Book of the Beginnings
Gerald Massey

volume one, Massey focuses on Egyptian origins in the British Isles. In the
cond volume, he explores the African/Egyptian roots of the Hebrews, the
kkado-Assyrians, and the Maori. By linking these diverse cultures and origins to
eir African roots, Massey demonstrates not only the extent of African influence
t its durability as well.
BN 0-933121-93-8. 1881*, 1995. 1200 pp. Two volume set. Cloth $84.95.

The Natural Genesis
Gerald Massey

y centralizing Egypt as the root of Western civilization's myths, symbols,
ligions, and languages, this famed Egyptologist and 'mythographer' challenges
nventions of theology as well as fundamental notions of race supremacy.
troduction by Dr. Charles S. Finch.
BN 1-57478-009-3. 1883*, 1998. 1087 pp. Two volume set. Paper $59.95.

Christianity, Islam and the Negro Race
Edward W. Blyden

lyden offers an early African-centered perspective on race, religion, and the
velopment of Africa.
BN 0-933121-41-5. 1887*, 1993. 441 pp. Paper $14.95.

To order, send a check or money order to:
Black Classic Press
P.O. Box 13414-b
Baltimore, MD 21203-3414

clude $5 for shipping and handling, and $.50 for each additional book ordered.
Credit card orders call: 1-800-476-8870

or a complete list of titles, please visit our website at www.blackclassic.com

ndicates first year published

www.ingramcontent.com/pod-product-compliance
Lightning Source LLC
Chambersburg PA
CBHW071342280526
45787CB00001B/192